CDM questions and answers: a practical approach

Second edition

Pat Perry

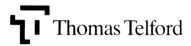
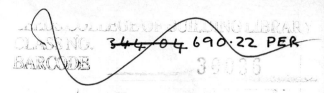

Thomas Telford

Published by Thomas Telford Publishing, Thomas Telford Ltd, 1 Heron Quay, London E14 4JD.
URL: http://www.thomastelford.com

Distributors for Thomas Telford books are
USA: ASCE Press, 1801 Alexander Bell Drive, Reston, VA 20191-4400, USA
Japan: Maruzen Co. Ltd, Book Department, 3–10 Nihonbashi 2-chome, Chuo-ku, Tokyo 103
Australia: DA Books and Journals, 648 Whitehorse Road, Mitcham 3132, Victoria

First edition published 1999
Second edition published 2002

A catalogue record for this book is available from the British Library

ISBN: 0 7277 3107 6

Typeset by MHL Typesetting Limited, Coventry.
Printed and bound in Great Britain by Bell & Bain Ltd, Glasgow.

Preface

This is the second and revised edition of the very successful first book, *CDM questions and answers: a practical approach.*

The Construction (Design and Management) Regulations 1994 (CDM Regulations) have now had many years to become integrated into construction projects and yet, for many clients and professionals, they still remain a mystery of jargon and ambiguity.

The Health and Safety Executive (HSE) has recognised a willingness on the part of the construction industry to improve standards of health and safety, yet understand that the legislation and associated Codes of Practice and Guidance are often confusing. Consequently, a Revised Approved Code of Practice has been issued, which came into force in February 2002. The Regulations themselves have not been changed (except for the definition of a designer, which was amended in 2000) but their interpretation has been revised to be better understood and more user-friendly.

This book refers to the Revised Approved Code of Practice and attempts to interpret pragmatically the intentions of CDM as expected by the HSE. A pre-publication copy of the Regulations was used as a guide and information is up to date as of November 2001.

In addition to referencing the Revised Approved Code of Practice: Managing Health and Safety in Construction (HSG 224), the layout of the book has been revised in order to address key stages of a project rather than key duties.

The book is now divided into five main parts covering:

- Part 1 — Introduction to Construction (Design & Management) Regulations 1994 and general health and safety
- Part 2 — Feasibility and design stage
- Part 3 — Proceeding to site
- Part 4 — On site
- Part 5 — Post construction.

At the beginning of each part, there is a general synopsis of what to find in the ensuing chapters.

The contents pages list questions in sequence for each chapter and all questions are listed alphabetically at the end of the book.

Appendices have been included to give examples of every day working forms and templates. These can be used as a basis for individual adaptation for specific user requirements.

Biography

Pat Perry, MCIEH, MIOSH, FRSH, MIIRM, qualified as an Environmental Health Officer in 1978 and spent the first years of her career in local government enforcing environmental health laws, in particular health and safety law, which became her passion. She has extensive knowledge of her subject and has served on various working parties on both health and safety and food safety. Pat contributes regularly to professional journals, e.g. *Facilities Business*, and has been commissioned by Thomas Telford Publishing to write a series of health and safety books.

After a period in the private sector, Pat set up her own environmental health consultancy, Perry Scott Nash Associates Ltd, in the latter part of 1988, and fulfilled her vision of a 'one-stop shop' for the provision of consultancy services to the commercial and retail sectors.

The consultancy has grown considerably over the years and provides consultancy advice to a wide range of clients in a variety of market sectors. Leisure and retail have become the consultancy's major expertise and the role of planning supervisor and environmental health consultant is provided on projects ranging from a few hundred thousand pounds to many millions, e.g. new public house developments and major department store re-fits and refurbishments.

Perry Scott Nash Associates Ltd has strong links to the enforcing agencies, consultants having come mostly from similar backgrounds and approach projects and all the issues and concerns associated with legal compliance with pragmatism and commercial understanding.

Should you wish to contact Pat Perry about any issue on this book, or to enquire further about the consultancy services offered by Perry Scott Nash Associates Ltd, please contact us direct at:

Perry Scott Nash Associates Ltd
Perry Scott Nash House
Primett Road
Stevenage
Herts
SG1 3EE

Alternatively phone, fax or e-mail on:

Tel: 01438 745771
Fax: 01438 745772
E-mail: p.perry@perryscottnash.co.uk

We would also recommend that you visit our website at:
www.perryscottnash.co.uk.

Acknowledgements

I would like to thank my Business Support Team at Perry Scott Nash Associates Ltd for their hard work and commitment in translating hand-written scripts into a typed, presentable manuscript and for their never failing patience as I change my mind, restructure, re-organise and re-write chapters. Well done Business Support Team.

I would also like to thank my Management Team for allowing me to take time out to complete the book and, in particular, Maureen, for her constant encouragement and support.

Glossary

CDM	Construction (Design and Management) Regulations 1994
Client	Organisation or individual for whom construction work is carried out
Client's Agent	Someone appointed by the Client to assume the responsibilities of 'Client' under the CDM Regulations and to act as if the Client
Cleaning Work	The cleaning of any window or any transparent or translucent wall, ceiling or roof in or on a structure where it involves a risk of a person falling more than two metres
Construction Phase Health and Safety Plan	A safety plan that has to be developed before the commencement of the construction phase by the Principal Contractor and which must set out the health and safety management arrangements for the project so that the safety of all persons involved is protected
Contractor	An organisation or individual who carries on a trade or business, or other undertaking, in connection with which he/she undertakes or carries out construction work, including sub-contractors
Construction work	Generally, the carrying out of building, civil engineering or engineering construction work. Regulation 2 CDM contains the full definition
Construction phase	The start of the construction works, including site preparations and any demolition

Demolition/ dismantling	The deliberate pulling down, destruction or taking apart of a structure or a substantial part of the structure, including dismantling and re-erection for re-use
Domestic Client	People who have work done that does not relate to their trade or profession, e.g. people commissioning building work on their own home
Duty Holder	Someone who has duties under the CDM Regulations 1994
Designer	Any individual or trade or business which involves them in preparing designs for construction work — e.g. preparing drawings, design details, specifications, bills of quantities and materials specifications
Developer	Someone who arranges for construction works to be carried out while acting on behalf of a domestic Client
Fragile material	A surface or an assembly that is liable to give way if a person or load crosses it, works on it or which will collapse if a load is dropped on to it
Hazard	Anything with the potential to cause harm to an individual, group of persons or damage to property
Health and Safety File	Information generated during the course of the construction project which future owners and occupiers of the building may need to know from a health and safety point of view
Maintenance	Repair, upkeep, redecoration of buildings, structures, plant and equipment. Includes cleaning with water or abrasives or cleaning with corrosive or toxic chemicals

Pre-tender Health and Safety Plan	The 'First Stage' Health and Safety Plan, prepared by the Planning Supervisor and forwarded to the Principal Contractor. The plan must include all information on the construction project relevant to significant health and safety risks. It should also address any environmental issues, e.g. contaminated land
Principal Contractor	The Main or Managing Contractor for a construction project appointed by the Client to assume the duties of Principal Contractor. The contractor responsible for the overall health and safety management of a site
Risk	The likelihood of a hazard being realised
Hierarchy of Risk Control	The principle of risk management, as follows. 1. Eliminate the hazard completely 2. Reduce the hazard to an acceptable level e.g. substitution 3. Control of the hazard/risk at source 4. Protect the individual 5. Monitor and review
Competency	Demonstration by an individual or organisation that they have sufficient experience, knowledge and other skills to carry out their duties satisfactorily
Resources	A general term including availability of the necessary plant, equipment, technical expertise, trained and competent people, and time with which to carry out construction projects and comply with CDM
Training	Formal instruction in health and safety matters, e.g. practical demonstrations on how to use plant and equipment, training in hazard awareness, etc.

Information   Any information which it is reasonable to
                     assume that an individual should know in
                     order to ensure that they discharge their duties
                     safely and protect the safety of others.

Contents

Part 1

Introduction to Construction (Design and Management) Regulations 1994 and general health and safety

Chapter summary

Chapter 1 The Construction (Design and Management) Regulations 1994 explained

Poses questions and answers on definitions, duties, duty holders, application of CDM to projects, notification to HSE, and fixed plant definitions.

Chapter 2 General health and safety

Contains questions and answers on health and safety legislation, other than CDM, applicable to building projects, and covers hazard and risk and the all important Management of Health & Safety at Work Regulations 1999.

1

The Construction (Design and Management) Regulations 1994 explained

What are the CDM Regulations and what is their purpose?

The CDM Regulations are the common name for the Construction (Design and Management) Regulations 1994, a set of Regulations which came into force on 31 March 1995.

The Regulations were introduced as a result of a European Union Directive detailing the minimum standards of health and safety at temporary or mobile construction sites (92/57/EEC).

The purpose of the Regulations is to improve the health and safety record on construction sites by requiring all parties involved in a construction project to take responsibility for health and safety standards. By requiring better planning, design and management of a construction project, it is believed that unacceptably high accident and fatality rates will be reduced.

The Regulations are also intended to help reduce the high incident rate of occupational ill-health, which is common in the construction industry, e.g. chronic respiratory conditions, muscular-skeletal conditions, industrial deafness, industrial dermatitis, etc.

Those who could create health and safety risks have been made responsible for considering and controlling them during all stages of the project — conception, design, planning, construction work, future maintenance and use of the building, including demolition.

Legislation

Construction (Design and Management) Regulations 1994 Implementation of Minimum Health & Safety Requirements at Temporary or Mobile Construction Sites (92/57/EEC).

The CDM Regulations refer to key appointments that must be made on a construction project. What does this mean?

The CDM Regulations identify four key 'posts' that have responsibilities for ensuring that health and safety matters are addressed during construction projects. They are:

The Client (or the Client's Agent)
The Designer
The Planning Supervisor
The Principal Contractor

The Client is anyone for whom a construction project is carried out.

The Designer is anyone who carries on a trade, business or undertaking in connection with which he:

● prepares a design, and
● includes any employee or other person at work, under his control, preparing it for him

relating to a structure or part of a structure.

The Planning Supervisor is a 'function' whereby the overall responsibility for co-ordinating health and safety aspects of the design and planning stage is undertaken.

The Principal Contractor must be a Contractor and must take responsibility for all site-specific safety issues, including ensuring that Contractors and Sub-contractors are competent and have resources to carry out the work safely, and that a Health and Safety Plan is developed. Principal Contractors are also responsible for providing information, training and consultation with employees, including the self-employed.

Legislation

Construction (Design and Management) Regulations 1994

- *Regulation 2*
- *Regulation 4*
- *Regulation 6*
- *Regulation 8*
- *Regulation 9*

Code of Practice

Managing Health and Safety in Construction (HSG 224: ISBN 0 7176 2139 1)

Guidance

A Guide to Managing Health and Safety in Construction (HSE: ISBN 0 7176 07550)

When does CDM apply?

The CDM Regulations apply to all construction work which falls into any of the following:

- lasts *more than* THIRTY (30) DAYS
- involves, or is *expected* to involve, more than FIVE HUNDRED (500) person days
- involves *more than* FOUR (4) people at work at any one time carrying out construction work
- involves *any* demolition or dismantling works (except where the Local Authority is the enforcing authority).

The Regulations apply to:

- new build construction
- alteration, maintenance and renovation of a structure
- site clearance
- demolition and dismantling of a structure
- temporary works.

Legislation

Construction (Design and Management) Regulations 1994

- *Regulation 3*

Code of Practice

Managing Health and Safety in Construction (HSG 224: ISBN 0 7176 2139 1)

Guidance

A Guide to Managing Health and Safety in Construction (HSE: ISBN 0 7176 07550)

What is 'construction work' under the CDM Regulations?

Construction work means the carrying out of building, civil engineering or engineering construction work.

The definition includes:

- the construction, alteration, conversion, fitting out, commissioning, renovation, repair, upkeep, redecoration or other maintenance (including cleaning that involves the use of water or an abrasive at high pressure or the use of substances classified as corrosive or toxic) decommissioning, demolition or dismantling of a structure

- the preparation for an intended structure, including site clearance, exploration, investigation (but not site survey), excavation, laying and installing the foundations of the structure
- the assembly of prefabricated elements to form a structure or the disassembly of prefabricated elements that previously formed a structure
- the removal of a structure or part of a structure or any product or waste resulting from demolition or dismantling of a structure or from the disassembly of prefabricated elements which, immediately before disassembly, formed a structure
- the installation, commissioning, maintenance repair or removal of mechanical, electrical, gas, compressed air, hydraulic, telecommunications, computer or similar services that are normally fixed within or to a structure and that involve a risk of falling more than two metres.

Legislation

Construction (Design and Management) Regulations 1994

- *Regulation 2*

Code of Practice

Managing Health and Safety in Construction (HSG 224: ISBN 0 7176 2139 1)

What is not 'construction work'?

The following activities are generally not classed as construction work:

- general horticultural work and tree planting
- archaeological investigations
- erecting and dismantling marquees

- erecting and dismantling lightweight partitions that divide open plan offices
- creation of exhibition stands and displays
- erection of scaffolds for support or access for work activities that are not classed as construction works
- site survey works, e.g. taking levels, assessing soil types and examining structures
- work to or on ships
- on-shore fabrication of elements for off-shore installations
- factory manufacture of items for use on construction sites.

Legislation

Construction (Design and Management) Regulations 1994

- *Regulation 2*

Code of Practice

Managing Health and Safety in Construction (HSG 224: ISBN 0 7176 2139 1)

The CDM Regulations refer to a 'notifiable project'. What is this?

The regulations require certain projects to be notified to the Health and Safety Executive (HSE) in the same way that the Factories Act 1961 required notification of building operations. (The Factories Act Section 127 (6 & 7) has been repealed by the CDM Regualtions 1994.)

A construction project is notifiable to the HSE area office when:

- it will, or is expected to, last more than THIRTY DAYS, or
- it will, or is expected to, involve more than FIVE HUNDRED PERSON DAYS.

The HSE require certain information that is outlined in Schedule 1 of the CDM Regulations. As long as the relevant information is given, it can be supplied in any format but, in order to facilitate notification, the HSE have produced Form F10 (rev) which can be used for all projects.

An example of Form F10 (rev) is shown in Appendix 1.

Legislation

Construction (Design and Management) Regulations 1994

● *Regulation 7*

Code of Practice

Managing Health and Safety in Construction (HSG 224: ISBN 0 7176 2139 1)

When does the construction phase start and are weekends and bank holidays counted?

The construction phase for the purposes of notification to the HSE is from the day 'construction works' start.

Remember, *site clearance* constitutes construction works and must be included in the calculation.

If construction work is programmed to take place on Saturdays and Sundays, and on any Bank Holiday, no matter how long the working shift will be, these days must be counted as 'construction days'.

Legislation

Construction (Design and Management) Regulations 1994

● *Regulation 3*

Code of Practice

Managing Health and Safety in Construction (HSG 224: ISBN 0 7176 2139 1)

What is a 'person day'?

A 'person day' is any day or part of a day (no matter how short) when someone is expected to carry out construction work. A person day relates to *one* individual and includes Site Agents, the Foreman, and Supervisors.

They do not actually have to be carrying out any physical work to be involved in 'construction work' — if they are managing the project they are included as a 'person day'.

Legislation

Construction (Design and Management) Regulations 1994

• *Regulation 3*

Code of Practice

Managing Health and Safety in Construction (HSG 224: ISBN 0 7176 2139 1)

Why do the HSE need to know about these projects?

The Health and Safety Executive (HSE) enforces health and safety laws in the construction industry. Projects lasting over 30 days are considered to be substantial building or refurbishment projects where the risks to health and safety of operatives and others can be high. The HSE has always been made aware of construction projects so that they can plan their inspection programme of enforcing the laws.

The HSE receive over 500,000 project notifications per year and use the notification process to help them target their on-site inspection priorities. In addition, they will review the F10s to try to influence the design process, enquiring about the provision for health and safety where appropriate.

Legislation

Construction (Design and Management) Regulations 1994

● *Regulation 7*

Code of Practice

Managing Health and Safety in Construction (HSG 224: ISBN 0 7176 2139 1)

What does the HSE do when they receive all these F10s?

The Construction division of the local HSE office records all forms received and allocates the projects to individual inspectors. The HSE inspectors base their routine inspections on the type of projects notified and will prioritise projects into perceived risk categories, e.g. those where falls from height are likely, or which involve excavations, etc.

The Construction Inspector, or the Administration Officer, will look at key dates on the form. They are interested to note when the form is signed by the Planning Supervisor and received by them, and when works are proposed to start on site.

If there are only a few days between the HSE receiving the form and works starting on site they will investigate because the essence of CDM is to involve the Planning Supervisor (and Designers) in the planning process of a project in respect of health and safety.

They will want to establish whether:

- the Client appointed a Planning Supervisor early enough in the project, i.e. as soon as he had information about the project and the construction work involved
- the Planning Supervisor notified the project to the HSE as soon as was practicable after their appointment.

A Client who fails to appoint a Planning Supervisor early enough in the project is guilty of an offence. Likewise, a Planning Supervisor who delays in notifying a project unreasonably is guilty of an offence.

It is not a valid excuse for either party to rely on the fact that financial resources had not been released for the project and, therefore, the project was not 'live'.

Legislation

Construction (Design and Management) Regulations 1994

- *Regulation 7*

Code of Practice

Managing Health and Safety in Construction (HSG 224: ISBN 0 7176 2139 1)

Guidance

CDM Regulations — Practical Guidance for Planning Supervisors (CIRIA Report 173)

Case Study

A Developer was undertaking 'core and shell' works for new retail units and had notified the HSE in the usual way. The shell unit went under offer to a restaurant company who commissioned their Designers to fit out the shell. The Developers work overran the time-scales and legal complications delayed the Client purchase. The Client appointed the Planning Supervisor as soon as the legal work had been completed and the shell building was handed over. The Client wanted works of fitting out to start as soon as possible. The Planning Supervisor notified the HSE on Form F10, indicating that works were due to start on site in approximately two weeks.

The HSE wrote to the Planning Supervisor to enquire at what date they were appointed and why notification was late. They asked to see letters of appointment for the Planning Supervisor with a view to determining whether the Client had failed in their duty to appoint the Planning Supervisor 'as soon as practicable after information about the project becomes available'.

If the Client had complied with his legal duty of an early appointment, the HSE wanted to establish whether the Planning Supervisor was dilatory in making the notification, thereby breaching their duties under Regulation 7.

In this instance, the HSE advised that, in their view, the Client had appointed the Planning Supervisor too late in the design process and that, in future, the Client should appoint the Planning Supervisor as soon as an intended purchase had been agreed.

What happens if a project is not notifiable but has more than four workers on site at any one time?

The project is *not* notifiable but CDM Regulations apply to the construction works, with the exception of Regulation 7: Notification of Project.

This means that the area HSE office will not receive formal notification of the construction project but this does not mean that they will not carry out a statutory inspection of the site. HSE inspectors have powers under the Health & Safety at Work Etc. Act 1974 to enter any 'premises' at all reasonable times to carry out their statutory duties.

Even though the construction project is not notifiable, health and safety legislation still applies to the project and the HSE Inspector has a duty to ensure that Contractors comply.

Legislation

Construction (Design and Management) Regulations 1994

● *Regulation 3*

Code of Practice

Managing Health and Safety in Construction (HSG 224: ISBN 0 7176 2139 1)

Guidance

A Guide to Managing Health and Safety in Construction (HSE: ISBN 0 7176 07550)

A project involves demolition work that will last three weeks and involves only four operatives. Presumably CDM will not apply?

No. CDM applies to *all* demolition works no matter how long the works last or how many operatives carry it out, with the exception of Regulation 7 — if the time-scales are less than 30 days or 500 person days.

The demolition works will not be notifiable unless they will last longer than 30 days or involve more than 500 person days.

Demolition does not include all works and does not include operations such as making holes in walls for window and door openings, removing non-structural internal walls or partitions, removing roof tiles, etc.

If the CDM Regulations do not apply to the project, other health and safety legislation does apply.

Legislation

Construction (Design and Management) Regulations 1994

● *Regulation 3 (3)*

Code of Practice

Managing Health and Safety in Construction (HSG 224: ISBN 0 7176 2139 1)

What happens if a project was originally going to last less than 30 days (or 500 person days) and not be notifiable but due to unforeseen circumstances it will now take longer?

Firstly, you must review *why* you thought it would be lasting less than 30 days in the first place. The Regulations state that where it is reasonable to assume that a project may take longer than 30 days (or 500 person days) it must be notified. The HSE will view seriously any intent to evade the Regulations by avoiding notification.

If the project is only to overrun by a few days, the HSE will not expect retrospective notification.

If the project will last a few more weeks, the Planning Supervisor should notify the HSE office on Form F10 and include a covering letter explaining the reasons for the project overrun and the late notification.

Legislation

Construction (Design and Management) Regulations 1994

● *Regulation 7*

Code of Practice

Managing Health and Safety in Construction (HSG 224: ISBN 0 7176 2139 1)

What does demolition and dismantling work include?

Demolition is taken to mean the deliberate pulling down, destruction or taking apart of a structure, or a substantial part of the structure.

Dismantling is the taking down, or taking apart, of all, or a substantial part of a structure, and includes situations where the structure is carefully taken down for re-use.

A 'structure' is defined as:

Any building, steel or re-enforced concrete structure (not being a building), railway line or siding, tramway line, dock, harbour, inland navigation, tunnel, shaft, bridge, viaduct, waterworks, reservoir, pipe or pipeline (whatever in either case it contains or is intended to contain) cable, aqueduct, sewer, sewerage works, gasholder, road, airfield, sea defence works, river works, drainage works, earthworks, lagoon, dam, wall, caisson, mast, tower, pylon, underground tank, earth retaining structure, or structures designed to preserve or alter any natural feature, and any other structure similar to the forgoing.

or

Any formwork, false work, scaffold or other structure designed or used to provide support or means of access during construction work.

or

Any fixed plant in respect of work which is installation, commissioning, de-commissioning, or dismantling and where any such work involves a risk of a person falling more than 2 metres.

The CDM Regulations apply to demolition and dismantling works irrespective of whether the project is notifiable and regardless of how many operatives are involved.

Legislation

Construction (Design and Management) Regulations 1994

● *Regulation 2*
● *Regulation 3*

Code of Practice

Managing Health and Safety in Construction (HSG 224: ISBN 0 7176 2139 1)

Is there a difference between 'demolition' and 'dismantling' works?

Demolition is the deliberate pulling down, destruction or taking apart of all, or a substantial part, of the structure.

Dismantling is the taking down, or taking apart, of all, or a substantial part, of a structure.

Dismantling for re-erection or re-use will be demolition for the purposes of CDM.

The formation of openings for windows, doors and services are not in themselves demolition works.

The removal of cladding, roof tiles or scaffolding is not, in itself, demolition or dismantling works unless included in, or combined with, other building operations.

Legislation

Construction (Design and Management) Regulations 1994

● *Regulation 3*

Code of Practice

Managing Health and Safety in Construction (HSG 224: ISBN 0 7176 2139 1)

Why do the Regulations always apply to demolition and dismantling works?

The health and safety risks associated with the demolition or dismantling of any structure are considerable and many accidents are caused through demolitions that have been poorly planned, ill-equipped and carried out by inexperienced people.

Whenever demolition works are involved, there is a risk of premature collapse. Designers must consider the risks to structural stability when specifying demolition.

Case Study

A small retailer is having a brick out-house demolished to make way for additional car parking. The building is single storey, single skin brickwork under a flat roof. The local builder can undertake the work in two days with three men on site.

The works involved fall within the definition of demolition and, irrespective of their duration and the number of operatives on site, the works come under the control of CDM.

The Client — the shop owner — has to comply with all the requirements of CDM except Regulation 7: Notification.

The Client appoints the builder as Planning Supervisor and Principal Contractor and discusses with him the use of the rear yard, the previous use of the out-house and whether he has any information as to how it was constructed.

The builder makes notes that the rear yard is used for access to the shop by delivery vehicles but it is not used as staff access, nor does anyone else have rights of access. The information on the building to be demolished is brick, single skin, and flat felt roof. No services are connected to the out building.

The builder prepares a combined Pre-tender and Construction Health and Safety Plan, which amounts to one page. He stipulates that the rear yard will be cordoned off, that the shop owner will reschedule deliveries for later in the week, after demolition, that the skip will be positioned away from the rear emergency exit door, that his operatives will be able to use the shop WC and tea-making facilities, and that waste will be removed by a licensed disposal company. In addition, the builder prepares a brief Method Statement covering the sequence of demolition, identifying hazards and risks, e.g. dust inhalation and falling from height (the structure is more than two metres high).

The shop owner is given a copy of the Health and Safety Plan and it is agreed before works start.

The Regulations place responsibilities on Clients, Designers and Contractors to manage the risks involved in demolition and dismantling, and to allow adequate competency and resources for carrying out the job.

Legislation

Construction (Design and Management) Regulations 1994

● *Regulation 3 (3)*

Code of Practice

Managing Health and Safety in Construction (HSG 224: ISBN 0 7176 2139 1)

What is cleaning work under CDM?

Specialist cleaning works involving high-pressure water, corrosive or toxic chemicals, e.g. stone cleaning, are included in the definition of 'construction works' and CDM Regulations may apply depending on the length of project and number of operatives.

Cleaning work means the cleaning of any window or any transparent or translucent wall, ceiling or roof in, or on, a structure where such cleaning involves a risk of a person falling more than two metres.

Day to day cleaning activities do *not* fall within the scope of CDM.

Designers have to make sure they consider the health and safety aspects of cleaning works, i.e. cleaning where there is a risk of falling two metres or more in their designs. They should avoid foreseeable risks to health and safety, i.e. design out unsafe means of access, specify reversible windows, etc.

The Designer's Risk Assessments and design criteria must be included in the Health and Safety File and information must be available as to safe access, safe methods of cleaning, etc.

Case Study

A major Contractor faces prosecution under the CDM Regulations 1994 for failing to comply with the requirement for a Construction Phase Health and Safety Plan covering the demolition of an existing building on the construction site. The demolition Contractor failed to comply with safe systems of work or good practice, and an unsafe procedure placed persons, other than his employees, at risk to their health and safety.

The demolition Contractor was also facing prosecution under general health and safety laws and also under CDM Regulations for failing to ensure that Sub-contractors had the competency to carry out and mange the construction works.

The Client must make sure that the information contained in the Health and Safety File is made available to whoever needs it.

Legislation

Construction (Design and Management) Regulations 1994

- *Regulation 2*
- *Regulation 3*
- *Regulation 13*

Code of Practice

Managing Health and Safety in Construction (HSG 224: ISBN 0 7176 2139 1)

Guidance

Designing for Health & Safety in Construction (HSE: ISBN 07176 08077)

How do the CDM Regulations apply to Term Maintenance contracts?

If the items of work in the maintenance contract can be carried out without disrupting the normal activities of the company, and if the Local Authority are the enforcing authority for health and safety, then CDM will not apply.

If the works are 'construction works' and involve five or more workers at any one time, then CDM Regulations apply to those aspects of the project.

If the works are 'construction works' and last more than 30 days or involve more than 500 person days then they will be notifiable and all CDM Regulations will apply.

Where some of the works are outside of the Regulations and some within it, it would be advisable to apply CDM to all of the works.

Projects involving term maintenance must be reviewed individually.

Legislation

Construction (Design and Management) Regulations 1994

● *Regulation 2*
● *Regulation 3*

Code of Practice

Managing Health and Safety in Construction (HSG 224: ISBN 0 7176 2139 1)

Are there any circumstances when CDM does *not* apply to construction works?

Yes. Where the project is *not* notifiable and has the Local Authority as the enforcing authority for health and safety law or the project involves people who are not 'at work'.

The Environmental Health Department of the Local Authority is responsible for ensuring that the laws of health and safety are enforced within the following working environments:

● offices, shops, hotels, public houses
● warehouses
● leisure facilities
● theatres
● miscellaneous premises.

Where construction work which is not notifiable takes place in the above premises and *does not interrupt* the normal activities in the premises and does not require separation of the construction activities from other activities or is the maintenance or removal of insulation on pipes, boilers or other parts of heating or water systems, then CDM Regulations do not apply.

A flow chart to help decide whether CDM applies to the work or not is shown in Appendix 2.

If people undertaking the construction project are not at work, then CDM may not apply. Such circumstances would be self-build groups building homes they will live in, and community service offenders projects. But if anyone is deemed to be employed, then CDM may apply.

Legislation

Construction (Design and Management) Regulations 1994

● *Regulation 3*

Code of Practice

Managing Health and Safety in Construction (HSG 224: ISBN 0 7176 2139 1)

What does interruption of normal activities mean?

If the building or renovation, repair or redecoration works allows people to carry out their normal work without being moved out of the building then their 'normal' activity is not interrupted.

If you need to move office workers to another office, or create a hoarding to shut off a work area and have people work elsewhere in the building, then their 'normal' activity *is* interrupted and CDM applies.

Works in a shop that prevent people, both staff and customers, having access to a department will come under CDM.

Case Study

A Contractor was employed to carry out minor repairs and refurbishments to a retail store. The work area was to be taped off but customers and staff could still move around the store without hindrance and it was concluded that normal work activity was not interrupted.

The Local Authority was the enforcing authority for health and safety within the store and ancillary office accommodation.

Works were scheduled to involve six operatives and to take twenty days, including weekends. It was therefore *not* notifiable under Regulation 7 CDM and, as it involved no disruption to normal work activity being carried out inside the shop, the Client, i.e. the shop owner, decided that CDM Regulations did not apply.

Works of redecoration that can take place while people are doing their usual job or while customers can walk around the work area will not come under CDM. The Local Authority will be responsible for enforcing the law for these works.

Legislation

Construction (Design and Management) Regulations 1994

● *Regulation 3*

Code of Practice

Managing Health and Safety in Construction (HSG 224: ISBN 0 7176 2139 1)

If the Local Authority are responsible for the premises and the works are minor, not disrupting normal work activity, do they have to be informed?

No. There is no requirement to notify the Local Authority that you are undertaking minor refurbishment works, etc., under the CDM Regulations. Do not forget that you may still need Building Regulations approval for some internal works, or you may need to consult the Fire Officer.

If the CDM Regulations do *not* apply, there are no duties with which you have to comply.

Even though CDM does not apply, other health and safety legislation may apply, namely, but not exhaustively, the following:

● The Health & Safety at Work Etc. Act 1974
● The Control of Asbestos at Work Regulations 1987
● The Noise at Work Regulations 1989
● The Electricity at Work Regulations 1989
● The Management of Health & Safety at Work Regulations 1999
● The Manual Handling Operations Regulations 1992

- The Personal Protective Equipment Regulations 1992
- The COSHH Regulations 1999
- The Reporting of Injuries, Diseases & Dangerous Occurrences Regulations 1995
- The Health & Safety (Safety Signs & Signals) Regulations 1996
- The Construction (Health, Safety & Welfare) Regulations 1996
- The Fire Precautions (Places of Work) Regulations 1997 (as amended 1999)
- The Confined Space Regulations 1997
- The Provision and Use of Work Equipment Regulations 1998
- The Lifting Operations & Lifting Equipment Regulations 1998
- The Construction (Head Protection) Regulations 1989.

Legislation

Construction (Design and Management) Regulations 1994

- *Regulation 3*

Code of Practice

Managing Health and Safety in Construction (HSG 224: ISBN 0 7176 2139 1)

Does CDM apply to emergency works?

In any emergency, the first priority is to make sure that the premises or structure is safe and without imminent risk to the health and safety of members of the public and others.

Once the making safe has been carried out, then CDM Regulations should be applied, i.e. the Client should make the appointment of a Planning Supervisor and Principal Contractor, as soon as is practicable.

Designers, once appointed, must fulfil their responsibilities under Regulation 13.

The Construction Phase Health and Safety Plan should be developed as soon as is practicable and, if time does not allow a written Plan to be completed before the emergency works take place, verbal discussions and agreement should be reached regarding key health and safety issues. If possible, the key issues should be written down and the body of the Plan can then be developed as the works progress.

Emergency works that are likely to be substantial will inevitably fall under the CDM Regulations. It would be wise to consult the local HSE office about any plans, etc., even if there is not time to prepare the paperwork.

Legislation

Construction (Design and Management) Regulations 1994

● *Regulation 3*

Do the Regulations apply to domestic house building or repairs?

If you commission a builder to build you a house for your own occupation then CDM Regulations do not apply, with the exception that Designers have to comply with their duties to design safely and Contractors have to notify the HSE of projects lasting 30 days or more, or 500 person days or more.

If you have a new conservatory, extension, loft conversion or similar, then CDM does not apply. If you have major renovations carried out, then CDM does not apply. Designers also have to comply with Regulation 13.

If you commission painters and decorators, then CDM does not apply.

If you commission a house to be built to sell it to someone else, then you are a developer and Regulations 6 and 8–12 of CDM apply.

Notification to the HSE needs to be given by the Contractor unless the works will take less than 30 days or involve less than 500 person days.

Legislation

Construction (Design and Management) Regulations 1994

- *Regulation 3*
- *Regulation 5*

Code of Practice

Managing Health and Safety in Construction (HSG 224: ISBN 0 7176 2139 1)

Who are domestic Clients?

Domestic Clients are Clients who have work done that does not relate to any trade, business or other undertaking. This is usually someone who commissions work on their own home, or the home of a family member.

No duties are placed on domestic Clients by CDM. Those working for the domestic Client may have duties.

Legislation

Construction (Design and Management) Regulations 1994

- *Regulation 2*
- *Regulation 3*

Code of Practice

Managing Health and Safety in Construction (HSG 224: ISBN 0 7176 2139 1)

What duties remain in respect of CDM when work is done for a domestic Client?

Contractors have to notify the HSE of all projects which are notifiable, i.e. which last more than 30 days or involve more than 500 person days.

Notification can be by any of the Contractors appointed and can be on Form F10.

Designers have duties under Regulation 13, i.e. they must have adequate regard to health and safety when preparing their designs and must provide health and safety information to the domestic Client.

Legislation

Construction (Design and Management) Regulations 1994

- *Regulation 3*
- *Regulation 7*
- *Regulation 13*

Code of Practice

Managing Health and Safety in Construction (HSG 224: ISBN 0 7176 2139 1)

How do the CDM Regulations apply to developers?

When a project is carried out for a domestic Client and that person enters into an agreement with a person who carries on a business, trade or undertaking (whether for profit or not) in connection with which:

- land or an interest in the land is granted or transferred to the domestic Client, and
- construction work will be carried out on the land, and

- following the construction work, the land will include premises which will be occupied as a residence

then that person arranging for the construction work to be carried out will be a developer under the CDM Regulations.

Regulations 6 and 8–12 of CDM will apply to the developer and *not* to the domestic Client, as the developer assumes the role of 'Client'.

Legislation

Construction (Design and Management) Regulations 1994

- *Regulation 5*

Code of Practice

Managing Health and Safety in Construction (HSG 224: ISBN 0 7176 2139 1)

What constitutes a 'developer' under CDM?

A developer is someone who carries on a trade, business or undertaking (whether for profit or not) in connection with which:

- land or an interest in land is granted or transferred to the Client, and
- the developer undertakes that construction work will be carried out.

In effect, a 'developer' is a commercial developer who sells domestic premises before a project is complete and arranges for construction work to be carried out.

Developers in this category include Housing Associations, self-build companies and other such bodies, whether they are profit making or not.

Legislation

Construction (Design and Management) Regulations 1994

- *Regulation 2*
- *Regulation 3*
- *Regulation 5*

Code of Practice

Managing Health and Safety in Construction (HSG 224: ISBN 0 7176 2139 1)

What are the consequences of failing to comply with the CDM Regulations?

All 'duty holders' have legal responsibilities under the CDM Regulations.

Health and safety legislation is triable 'either way', i.e. either on summary conviction or on indictment. This means prosecutions can be heard in the Magistrates' Court or in the Crown Court.

If prosecutions are brought in the Magistrates' Court for contraventions of CDM Regulations then the maximum fine per offence is £5000. If prosecutions are brought in the Crown Court then fines are unlimited and custodial sentences are possible.

Any of the following can be prosecuted if they fail to discharge their legal duties:

- the Client
- the Planning Supervisor
- the Principal Contractor
- the Designers
- the Contractors.

Legislation

Construction (Design and Management) Regulations 1994
Health & Safety at Work Etc. Act 1974

Case Study

Following an investigation into two accidents, one a fatality, which happened on a construction site in London, the HSE brought a prosecution against the Principal Contractor for failing to have an adequate Construction Phase Health and Safety Plan in operation over the period of the two accidents.

The HSE also prosecuted the ground works Contractor for failing to take all reasonable steps to ensure that an excavation did not collapse accidentally and for failing to take suitable and sufficient measures to prevent vehicles overrunning the edge of an earthwork.

The Construction Phase Health and Safety Plan failed to consider the hazards and risks of the ground works, and did not include Risk Assessments and suitable Method Statements.

The prosecutions were heard in the Crown Court due to the severity of the accidents and the Principal Contractor was fined £20 000 plus £3000 costs. The ground works Contractor was fined a total of £20 000 for two charges under the Construction (Health, Safety and Welfare) Regulations 1996, plus £3000 costs.

What civil liability extends to the CDM Regulations?

The CDM Regulations constitute criminal law — it is a criminal act to contravene them. Anyone who does so incurs a criminal record.

Civil law applies to situations where an individual can sue another person (or a corporate body) for damages due to their negligence, i.e. failing in their common law duty of care.

Being prosecuted for criminal offences under CDM does not infer an automatic right to bring civil proceedings. A successful prosecution does not necessarily imply a failure in the duty of care under civil law and a successful civil case will depend on the facts of the case.

However, if a Principal Contractor is prosecuted for failing to satisfactorily ensure that unauthorised persons are prevented from entering the construction site, then Regulation 21 CDM confers a right to civil action.

Similarly, if a Client allows works to start on site without a satisfactory Construction Phase Health and Safety Plan and an accident ensues, the person injured will have the right to bring proceedings in the Civil Court.

Legislation

Construction (Design and Management) Regulations 1994

- *Regulation 10*
- *Regulation 16*
- *Regulation 21*

A separate demolition and making safe contract is to be let to a specialist Contractor before progressing the design options for the building. Do the CDM Regulations apply?

The CDM Regulations apply to *all* demolition works. 'Making Safe' works often involve demolition works as well as construction work, i.e. construction, alteration, renovation, repair, upkeep or maintenance and, therefore, the works fall within the definition of construction works under Regulation 3 CDM.

Therefore, the Client must appoint a Planning Supervisor and Principal Contractor for the demolition and making safe contract. There must be a Pre-tender and Construction Phase Health and Safety Plan, and a Health and Safety File.

Unless the initial works are going to last more than 30 days or involve more than 500 person days of construction works, they will *not* be notifiable. In order to qualify for non-notification, the works must form a discrete package that has an identifiable beginning and end. There must be a distinct break in the works — where one project ends before another one starts — so there is a complete break in all construction works.

If there is any doubt about how long the project will last and when one contract ends and another one starts, it is advisable to notify the entire project to the local HSE office.

An important Regulation to consider carefully is Regulation 8 — Competency of the Contractor. Demolition and making safe works are particularly hazardous and the HSE will be looking to ensure that an experienced, competent Contractor is appointed to manage the works.

Once the demolition and making safe package has ended, the duties of the appointed Planning Supervisor and Principal Contractor will cease. They can, however, be re-appointed to the main contract if their competency and resources are suitable.

A new Planning Supervisor and Principal Contractor can be appointed to the subsequent phases of the project.

Legislation

Construction (Design and Management) Regulations 1994

- *Regulation 3*
- *Regulation 6*

- *Regulation 8*
- *Regulation 9*

Code of Practice

Managing Health and Safety in Construction (HSG 224: ISBN 0 7176 2139 1)

Is work on fixed plant subject to CDM?

The installation, commissioning, decommissioning and dismantling of fixed plant is subject to CDM where persons are at risk of falling two metres or more.

The maintenance of fixed plant is not covered by CDM unless the work is part of a bigger package of refurbishment work.

If fixed plant is connected to mechanical, electrical and similar services, or is supported on a separate structure and work is required to these areas, then that work is likely to fall under CDM, as it falls within the definition of 'construction work'.

Legislation

Construction (Design and Management) Regulations 1994

- *Regulation 2*
- *Regulation 3*

Code of Practice

Managing Health and Safety in Construction (HSG 224: ISBN 0 7176 2139 1)

2

General health and safety

Are the CDM Regulations the only legislation applicable to construction projects?

No. A wide range of health and safety legislation applies to construction projects especially where there are employers, employees and self-employed persons involved. Also, the laws of health and safety apply to 'persons in control of premises' and this could mean that the Client has some responsibilities for safety.

The Health and Safety at Work Etc. Act 1974 is the key piece of legislation applicable to all people 'at work' and to others who may 'resort' to premises. Under the umbrella of the Health and Safety at Work Etc. Act 1974 are many subsidiary regulations that could apply to construction projects. Some of these are:

- Noise at Work Regulations 1989
- Control of Asbestos at Work Regulations 1987
- The Electricity at Work Regulations 1989
- The Manual Handling Operations Regulations 1992
- The Personal Protective Equipment Regulations 1992
- The Reporting of Injuries, Diseases and Dangerous Occurrences Regulations 1995
- The Construction (Health, Safety and Welfare) Regulations 1996
- The Health & Safety (Safety Signs and Signals) Regulations 1996
- The Fire Precautions (Place of Work) Regulations 1997 and 1999
- The Confined Spaces Regulations 1997
- The Provision and Use of Work Equipment Regulations 1998
- The Lifting and Lifting Operations Regulations 1998

- The Control of Substances Hazardous to Health Regulations 1999
- The Management of Health & Safety at Work Regulations 1999
- Construction (Head Protection) Regulations 1989.

What health and safety legislation (other than CDM) is the most important on a construction project?

All health and safety legislation is important and failure to comply with any relevant legislation is an offence punishable by a fine and/ or imprisonment.

All members of the project team should be aware of which legislation applies to the project and, in particular, the Principal Contractor must have detailed knowledge of what is relevant to the site and proposed works.

The main pieces of legislation applicable to construction sites are the Construction (Health, Safety and Welfare) Regulations 1996 and the Management of Health & Safety at Work Regulations 1999.

The Construction (Health, Safety and Welfare) Regulations 1996 set out general and specific requirements for maintaining health and safety on construction sites and cover issues such as:

- provision of welfare facilities
- working at heights
- traffic routes and pedestrians
- working in excavations
- working on platforms
- safe places of work
- falling objects
- demolition and dismantling
- prevention of drowning
- stability of structures
- fire safety
- emergency procedures
- housekeeping
- training
- statutory inspections.

The Management of Health & Safety at Work Regulations 1999 set out the principles for risk assessments, consultation with employees, co-operation, competency, information instruction and training. The CDM Regulations interact with these Regulations, particularly in respect of the Principal Contractor's duties under Regulations 16 and 17. Specific reference is also made in respect of Contractors' duties under Regulation 19.

The Principal Contractor is responsible primarily for ensuring health and safety on the construction site and must ensure that Contractors and Sub-contractors follow the requirements of the law. Where work activity on a site affects more than one Contractor, the Principal Contractor must take an overview and assess the risks to health and safety for all operatives.

Legislation

Construction (Health, Safety and Welfare) Regulations 1996
Management of Health & Safety at Work Regulations 1999

Code of Practice

Managing Health and Safety in Construction (HSG 224: ISBN 0 7176 2139 1)

What is 'hazard' and 'risk' in relation to health and safety?

Hazard means the potential to cause harm. *Risk* means the likelihood that harm will occur. A typical *hazard* on a construction site is falling from heights. The *risk* of falling is dependent on what control measures have been implemented, e.g.:

● the risk of falling is less if guard rails are provided
● the risk of falling is less if safety harnesses are used
● the risk of falling is less if safe means of access are provided — stairs and not ladders, tower scaffolds and not ladders, etc.

- the risk of falling is less if materials do not need to be carried
- the risk of falling is less if wind and weather conditions are considered
- the risk of falling is less if adequate working space is provided, e.g. not perched on a ledge.

The *hazard* of falling from heights will be high but the *risk* of falling will be low if guardrails are used.

Legislation

Construction (Design and Management) Regulations 1994

- *Regulation 13*

Management of Health & Safety at Work Regulations 1999

- *Regulation 3*

Code of Practice

Managing Health and Safety in Construction (HSG 224: ISBN 0 7176 2139 1)

Guidance

Five Steps to Risk Assessment (HSE INDG 163)
Five Steps to Risk Assessment — Case Studies (HSE HSG 183)
Designing for Health & Safety in Construction (HSC/CIAC)
CDM Regulations — Guidance for Designers (CIRIA Report 145)

What aspects of the Management of Health and Safety at Work Regulations 1999 apply to construction projects?

The Management of Health and Safety at Work Regulations 1999 (MHSWR) set out general duties for employers and employees in all non-domestic work activities and aim to improve health and safety management by developing the general principles set out in the Health and Safety at Work Etc. Act 1974.

The duties set out in MHSWR overlap with duties contained in several other pieces of health and safety legislation by developing the general principles set out in the Health and Safety at Work Etc. Act 1974.

Compliance with other legislation normally implies compliance with MHSWR but sometimes the duties in MHSWR go beyond those of other regulations. In these instances, the duties imposed by MHSWR take precedence over others.

MHSWR places duties on employers (and the self-employed), including Clients, Designers, Planning Supervisors, Principal Contractors and other Contractors.

Under MHSWR employers must:

- assess the risks to the health and safety of their employees and others who may be affected by the work activity (Regulation 3)
- identify what actions are necessary to eliminate or reduce the risks to health and safety of their employees and others
- apply the principles of prevention and protection
- carry out and record in writing, if they have five employees or more, a risk assessment
- make appropriate arrangements for managing health and safety, including planning, organisation, control, monitoring and review of preventative and protective measures — arrangements must be recorded if five or more employees
- provide appropriate health surveillance for employees whenever the risk assessment shows it necessary, e.g. to check for skin dermatitis
- appoint competent persons to assist with the measures needed to comply with health and safety laws — competent persons should ideally be from within the employer's own organisation and where more than one competent person is appointed the employer must ensure that adequate co-operation exists between them

- set up procedures to deal with emergencies and liaise, if necessary, with medical and rescue services
- provide employees with relevant information on health and safety in an understandable form
- co-operate with other employers sharing a common workplace and co-ordinate preventative and protective measures for the benefit of all employees and others
- make sure that employees are not given tasks beyond their capabilities and competence
- ensure that employees are given suitable training
- ensure that any temporary workers are provided with relevant health and safety information in order to carry out their work safely.

Employers have duties under MHSWR to:

- use equipment in accordance with training and instruction
- report dangerous situations
- report any shortcomings in health and safety arrangements
- take reasonable care of their own and other's health and safety.

The Principal Contractor will carry the bulk of the responsibility for MHSWR on a construction site and, as the site will be 'multi-occupied', the Principal Contractor must ensure co-operation and co-ordination between employers. This will be laid out in the Construction Phase Health and Safety Plan. Contractors must carry out their own risk assessments but the Principal Contractor must complete these where hazards and risks affect the whole workforce, e.g. site access routes and communal lifting operations. As a multi-occupied site, the Principal Contractor will assume overall responsibility for the management of health and safety and will co-ordinate and arrange emergency procedures, etc. Information on such procedures must be given to all persons using the site by the Principal Contractor. Information must be comprehensible and understandable, so it may need to be in picture form, cartoons, posters and foreign language, etc.

Legislation

Construction (Design and Management) Regulations 1994

- *Regulation 15*
- *Regulation 16*
- *Regulation 17*
- *Regulation 18*

Management of Health & Safety at Work Regulations 1999

- *All regulations*

Code of Practice

Managing Health and Safety in Construction (HSG 224: ISBN 0 7176 2139 1)
Management of Health and Safety at Work ACOP (HSE L21)

Part 2

Feasibility and design stage

Chapter summary

Chapter 3 The Client

Contains questions and answers on the role and responsibility of the Client during the design and feasibility of a project.

Chapter 4 The Planning Supervisor

A critical time for the Planning Supervisor to be involved in construction projects, this chapter looks at the roles, duties and responsibilities of the function.

Chapter 5 The Designer

Again, a critical role for the Designer during the initial design stage to contribute huge influence to the overall safety of the design and construction of the building. Questions covering Design Risk Assessments, information and surveys, specification of fragile materials, etc.

Chapter 6 The Principal Contractor

Usually less involvement at this stage for the Principal Contractor but if appointed early enough can make significant contribution to design discussions on feasibility. Questions on who can be Principal Contractor, duties, etc., are covered.

3

The Client

Who is a Client?

A Client is any person or company who is involved in a business, trade or undertaking for whom a construction project is carried out.

To fall into the definition of Client, it is not necessary for the construction works to actually take place, but the term refers to any person or company who first thinks about having a structure built, repaired, refurbished, demolished or maintained.

Concept and feasibility schemes are commissioned by a 'Client' under CDM and even though actual construction work may not take place, the principles of CDM must be applied.

Legislation

Construction (Design and Management) Regulations 1994

● *Regulation 2*

Code of Practice

Managing Health and Safety in Construction (HSG 224: ISBN 0 7176 2139 1)

Guidance

A Guide to Managing Health and Safety in Construction (HSE: ISBN 0 7176 07550)
Designing for Health & Safety in Construction (HSC/CIAC)

Why do CDM Regulations have to apply to Clients?

Research by the HSE over the years has revealed that Clients have tremendous influence on the planning, organisation and implementation of a construction project. If the Client has a cavalier attitude to health and safety, then it is likely that everyone on the project will develop a similar approach.

The CDM Regulations introduced for the first time legal responsibilities for Clients in respect of ensuring provision is made for health and safety on construction projects.

Legislation

Construction (Design and Management) Regulations 1994

- *Regulation 4*
- *Regulation 11*
- *Regulation 12*

Code of Practice

Managing Health and Safety in Construction (HSG 224: ISBN 0 7176 2139 1)

What are my duties as a Client under CDM Regulations?

The following duties must be carried out for every project to which CDM applies:

- appoint a Planning Supervisor
- appoint a Principal Contractor
- appoint competent Designers and other professionals to the Project Team
- ensure that resources to be provided by the Design Team and other appointments are adequate

- provide health and safety information about the project to the Planning Supervisor, including information on the site
- ensure a suitable Construction Phase Health and Safety Plan is approved *before* construction works start
- retain the Health and Safety File and make it available to whoever may need it in the future.

Legislation

Construction (Design and Management) Regulations 1994

- *Regulation 4*
- *Regulation 8*
- *Regulation 9*
- *Regulation 10*
- *Regulation 11*
- *Regulation 12*

Code of Practice

Managing Health and Safety in Construction (HSG 224: ISBN 0 7176 2139 1)

Guidance

CDM Regulations — Practical Guidance for Clients and Client's Agents (CIRIA Report 172)
A Guide to Managing Health and Safety in Construction (HSE: ISBN 0 7176 07550)

Why does a Planning Supervisor need to be appointed and what are they supposed to do?

The CDM Regulations create a new function of Planning Supervisor to help co-ordinate the health and safety aspects of a project and to undertake specific duties.

A Planning Supervisor can be an individual or a number of individuals, e.g. a company with health and safety experience and knowledge, construction and design knowledge and experience of project planning.

A good Planning Supervisor will ensure that your duties as a Client under the Regulation are being met, that your Designers fulfil their responsibilities and that the Principal Contractor manages site safety issues.

Effective co-ordination and planning will mean a more efficient project with reduced hazards and risks, better safety management, less lost time for accidents and a greater efficiency in respect of resources and time management.

The benefit of the Planning Supervisor can be determined by analysing the two words — planning and supervisor.

Planning — to make plans, i.e. a method or course of action thought out in advance especially in relation to the controlled design of buildings and development of land.

Supervisor — a person who manages or supervises, i.e. directs or oversees the performance or operation of a task, function etc.

Therefore, a good Planning Supervisor helps to ensure that health and safety is thought out in advance and that others involved in the project are directed or inspected in respect of their knowledge, approach and implementation of health and safety issues.

Planning Supervisors need to be competent and have adequate resources to do the job. They must have a comprehensive knowledge of the construction process and health and safety. They should not make the project more difficult or complicated. They should not create mounds of paperwork. They should not be obstructive.

Planning Supervisors should be helpful, give advice, co-ordinate, encourage, question, compromise, cajole and communicate with all members of the Design Team on *any* issue relating to health and safety of the project.

Legislation

Construction (Design and Management) Regulations 1994

● *Regulation 6*

Code of Practice

Managing Health and Safety in Construction (HSG 224: ISBN 0 7176 2139 1)

Guidance

A Guide to Managing Health and Safety in Construction (HSE: ISBN 0 7176 07550)
Designing for Health & Safety in Construction (HSE: ISBN 0 7176 08077)

What does the term 'Client's Agent' mean?

The Regulations permit a Client to hand over all their legal responsibilities under CDM to another person — known as the Client's Agent.

The Client's Agent becomes legally responsible for all the Client's duties and must perform them as if he were the Client.

A declaration that a Client's Agent has been appointed must be made to the area HSE office and Form F10 (rev) can be used. The declaration must be signed by the person appointed as the Client's Agent, and must include an address where any legal documents may be served.

It may be appropriate where several Clients are developing a multi-occupied site for them to designate one Client as Client's Agent so that there is clarity and consistency in the approach and implementation of the CDM Regulations.

If the Client's Agent breaks the law, in particular the duties placed on Clients made under CDM, the original Client may still be liable to prosecution if it can be proved that he appointed a person who was not competent to carry out the role of Client's Agent.

Any Client proposing to appoint a Client's Agent should assess the competency of the person so chosen and should request written information about health and safety attitudes, experience, competency and resources.

It would be sensible to appoint the person by way of a formal contract, specifically outlining what they are expected to be responsible for legally, and to require a signed and dated copy of the Contract before formal acceptance.

An example of a Client's Agent questionnaire is shown in Appendix 3 and an example of a formal agreement is shown in Appendix 4.

Legislation

Construction (Design and Management) Regulations 1994

● *Regulation 4*

Code of Practice

Managing Health and Safety in Construction (HSG 224: ISBN 0 7176 2139 1)

Guidance

A Guide to Managing Health and Safety in Construction (HSE: ISBN 0 7176 07550)

CDM Regulations — Practical Guidance for Clients and Client's Agents (CIRIA Report 172)

Client's Agent sounds like a good idea as responsibility for CDM will be delegated — can it be done for all projects?

Yes it can, provided that you can find someone who is prepared to assume your Client responsibilities.

When you appoint a Client's Agent you must make sure that they are competent to perform their duties, i.e. to discharge their duties as a Client.

You could appoint the Architect or Project Manager as Client's Agent, or another Client on a multi-Client job as your Agent. Whoever you appoint, you must give them authority to act in respect of your duties under the Regulations. Formal declarations must be signed and lodged with the HSE and Form F10 can be used.

You may not be responsible for the duties placed on a Client if you appoint a Client's Agent but the Courts may still consider that you have some responsibility should either a criminal or civil case ensue. Sections 36 and 37 of the Health & Safety at Work Etc. Act 1974 enable the HSE to prosecute anyone, including company directors etc., who have, by their own act, default, or connivance, caused the offence.

Legislation

Construction (Design and Management) Regulations 1994

● *Regulation 4*

Health & Safety at Work Etc. Act 1974

● *Section 36*
● *Section 37*

Code of Practice

Managing Health and Safety in Construction (HSG 224: ISBN 0 7176 2139 1)

Guidance

A Guide to Managing Health and Safety in Construction (HSE: ISBN 0 7176 07550)
CDM Regulations — Practical Guidance for Clients & Client's Agents (CIRIA Report 172)

What information must be provided to the Planning Supervisor?

In order to comply with your duties under CDM, you must ensure that the Planning Supervisor is provided with all relevant information in order for him to carry out his duties.

Relevant information will enable the Planning Supervisor to ensure that the Pre-tender Health and Safety Plan is prepared, and that the Designers are advised of key information to help them complete their Design Risk Assessments.

Examples of information a Client is expected to be able to provide:

- site details:
  - address of site
  - owner of site if different from Client
  - nature of project
  - commencement and duration of works

- appointments made by Client:
  - Architects
  - Quantity Surveyors
  - Structural Engineers
  - Specialist Designers
  - Project Managers
  - Principal Contractor (if known)

- location of site:
  - environmental information
  - proximity to roads, houses, schools, etc.

○ proximity to rivers, overhead power cables, power sub stations, etc.

● site boundaries:
   ○ demarcation/demise area
   ○ fencing and boundaries
   ○ ownership of adjoining land/premises
   ○ details of 'communal' shared area

● condition of structure:
   ○ description of building
   ○ state of dilapidation
   ○ structural information
   ○ fragile materials

● good conditions:
   ○ ground type
   ○ ground stability
   ○ contamination
   ○ presence of underground tanks, channels, pits, etc.

● location of mains services:
   ○ gas
   ○ electrical/power
   ○ telephone
   ○ communications
   ○ fuel supplies
   ○ overhead power lines

● hazardous substances:
   ○ asbestos
   ○ lead paint
   ○ dust/fumes
   ○ pigeon/rodent contamination
   ○ chemical contamination, e.g. oils and petrol

● overlap with Clients Undertaking:
   ○ employees still at work, e.g. any hazardous processes, hazardous areas, traffic routes and site safety rules

● existing Health and Safety File.

Legislation

Construction (Design and Management) Regulations 1994

● *Regulation 11*

Code of Practice

Managing Health and Safety in Construction (HSG 224: ISBN 0 7176 2139 1)

Do detailed surveys need to be commissioned in order to provide this information?

The more information available at the planning stage of the project regarding potential health and safety issues, the more likely it will be that the project can be programmed efficiently and safely.

Finding out about the presence of hazardous substances, e.g. asbestos once the construction phase has started means downtime, costs and potential health risks to all operatives and others. Breaches of legislation are inevitable.

It makes sound business sense to obtain as much information about the site before progressing the design phase. Asking a Structural Engineer to advise on load bearing walls and the necessary temporary works will prevent a major on-site collapse, which could cause major and fatal injuries to those on site.

Commissioning the following would not be unreasonable:

● building survey including services
● structural survey
● asbestos and other hazardous substance survey
● pest survey
● contaminated land survey
● environmental noise survey.

The CDM Regulations are about reducing hazards and risks to health and safety, i.e. being prepared to deal with what is there because of being forewarned.

If asbestos is present it poses a *serious* health hazard. The HSE expects all Clients to have identified the existence of asbestos on site *before* construction works start and to have included proposals to deal with it in the Pre-tender Health and Safety Plan, e.g. remove it completely or encapsulate it, label it and manage the risks. (A preferred option is always to remove asbestos from site following the legal requirements of the Control of Asbestos at Work Regulations 1987.)

Each project needs to be assessed on its merits — if the building is a new 'developers' shell' then detailed surveys will not be necessary, as the developer will have dealt with these issues. If the building is post-1980 it is unlikely (though not guaranteed) that it will have sprayed asbestos coating and lagging as insulation and fire protection material but it may have asbestos boards or asbestos cement tiles.

A high street retail premises that has been in existence for decades may not need a contaminated land survey unless a review of previous planning permissions indicates an industrial factory or petrol station had been present on the site.

Legislation

Construction (Design and Management) Regulations 1994

● *Regulation 11*

Code of Practice

Managing Health and Safety in Construction (HSG 224: ISBN 0 7176 2139 1)

Can the responsibility of providing information be delegated to someone else?

Yes. It would seem sensible for the Client to delegate the commissioning and interpretation of surveys and reports to either the Project Manager or Project Architect.

It would be helpful to provide a list of information you expect to be made available for the project and to agree budget costs for securing the surveys.

Legislation

Construction (Design and Management) Regulations 1994

● *Regulation 11*

Code of Practice

Managing Health and Safety in Construction (HSG 224: ISBN 0 7176 2139 1)

4

The Planning Supervisor

What is the Planning Supervisor in respect of the CDM Regulations?

The Planning Supervisor is an appointment that the Client must make to ensure that health and safety is co-ordinated during the design and planning phase of the project.

The Planning Supervisor need not be an individual person. The function can be discharged by several bodies if appropriate, i.e. specialist input at each stage of the design and planning process, and the responsibilities of the post can be shared.

The Planning Supervisor should be a member of the Design Team, as it is felt that many health and safety issues relating to construction projects, and subsequent maintenance tasks, can be 'designed out' in the design and planning process.

The Planning Supervisor is expected to have influence over the Design Team (and Client) and to highlight health and safety issues, and to initiate discussions regarding ways to implement the 'Hierarchy of Risk Control'.

The Planning Supervisor is expected to co-ordinate information relating to health and safety among the Design Team and to facilitate the sharing of information so that a holistic approach to health and safety on the project is achieved.

Legislation

Construction (Design and Management) Regulations 1994

- *Regulation 6*
- *Regulation 14*

Code of Practice

Managing Health and Safety in Construction (HSG 224: ISBN 0 7176 2139 1)

Guidance

A Guide to Managing Health and Safety in Construction (HSE: ISBN 0 7176 07550)
CDM Regulations — Practical Guidance for Planning Supervisors (CIRIA Report 173)

What are the key duties of a Planning Supervisor?

The Planning Supervisor has overall responsibility for co-ordinating the health and safety aspects of the design and planning phase and for the early stages of the Health and Safety Plan and for ensuring that the Health and Safety File is produced.

The Planning Supervisor must ensure that Designers have given adequate regard to health and safety within their design, in particular that they have:

- avoided foreseeable risks to the health and safety of any person at work carrying out construction work or cleaning work in or on the structure at any time, or of any person who may be affected by the work of such a person at work
- combated at source risks to the health and safety of any person at work carrying out construction work or cleaning work in or on the structure at any time, or of any person who may be affected by the work of such a person at work
- given priority to measures which will protect all persons at work who may carry out construction work or cleaning work at any

time and all persons who may be affected by the work of such a person at work over measures which only protect each person carrying out such work.

As Planning Supervisor you have to ensure that the Designer has followed the 'Hierarchy of Risk Control'.

The Planning Supervisor must ensure that Designers co-operate with one another, as far as it is necessary for each of them to comply with the requirements of Regulation 13.

Other key duties include ensuring that the Health and Safety Plan is developed in respect of the project before the Contractor makes arrangements to carry out the work, i.e. that a Pre-tender (or pre-negotiation or pre-appointment) Health and Safety Plan is drawn up which gives the Contractor important information in respect of health and safety issues for the project.

A Health and Safety File must be produced for the project and the Planning Supervisor must ensure that this is done and handed over to the Client. In addition, the Planning Supervisor must review, attend or add to the Health and Safety File as necessary so as to ensure it contains all relevant information when handed over to the Client.

An important duty of the Planning Supervisor is to give adequate advice to any Client or Contractor so as to enable them to comply with their duties under Regulations 8 and 9 in competency and resources, and to provide adequate advice to a Client in respect of Regulation 10 — advising on the adequacy of the Construction Phase Health and Safety Plan.

Finally, the Planning Supervisor has to notify the project to the relevant HSE office on Form F10 or similar.

Legislation

Construction (Design and Management) Regulations 1994

- *Regulation 7*
- *Regulation 14*

Code of Practice

Managing Health and Safety in Construction (HSG 224: ISBN 0 7176 2139 1)

Guidance

A Guide to Managing Health and Safety in Construction (HSE: ISBN 0 7176 07550)
CDM Regulations — Practical Guidance for Planning Supervisors (CIRIA Report 173)

The CDM Regulations use the word 'ensure' in respect of the Planning Supervisor's duties. Does this mean that the Planning Supervisor has actually to carry out the tasks?

No. Strict interpretation of the Regulations only requires the Planning Supervisor to ensure that the Health and Safety Plan is developed for the project, both before works are tendered or negotiated, and before construction works start. As long as the Health and Safety Plan was produced, the law would be complied with, regardless of who prepared the Plan.

Notwithstanding the above, the Approved Code of Practice indicates that it is the responsibility of the Planning Supervisor to 'prepare and develop' the Health and Safety Plan.

In the same way, the Planning Supervisor has to 'ensure' that the Health and Safety File is developed but does not actually have to do it, although the Planning Supervisor does have a legal responsibility to 'review, amend or add' to the Health and Safety File.

'Ensuring' that the Health and Safety Plan has been prepared for the project before a Contractor makes arrangements to carry out the construction work could be achieved by the Planning Supervisor checking that key health and safety information has been included in the Bill of Quantities, Project Specification or other Project Brief.

The actual information could be collated by the Designers and checked by the Planning Supervisor. If the Principal Contractor is brought into the project early, such as on a 'partnering' basis, the Principal Contractor could draw up the Pre-tender Health and Safety Plan for checking and agreement by the Planning Supervisor.

As the Planning Supervisor carries statutory responsibility for ensuring that a Health and Safety Plan is prepared, many Planning Supervisors consider it to be too important a task to delegate, and therefore they 'ensure' it is prepared by doing it themselves.

Legislation

Construction (Design and Management) Regulations 1994

- *Regulation 7*
- *Regulation 14*

Code of Practice

Managing Health and Safety in Construction (HSG 224: ISBN 0 7176 2139 1)

Guidance

A Guide to Managing Health and Safety in Construction (HSE: ISBN 0 7176 07550)

CDM Regulations — Practical Guidance for Planning Supervisors (CIRIA Report 173)

When does the Planning Supervisor have to notify the HSE?

As soon as the Planning Supervisor is appointed to the project and determines that the project is notifiable, they should notify the relevant HSE office of the construction project.

All the relevant information needed for the notification form may not be known at the time of the Planning Supervisor's appointment. This need not delay the Planning Supervisor's making the notification — tick the initial notification box in Form F10.

As soon as further information is available, e.g. confirmed start on site date, name of Principal Contractor, tick the 'additional notification' box in Form F10 and send the more detailed form to the HSE.

Make sure that either the 'initial' or 'additional' box is clearly indicated. The HSE uses F10s to assess project complexity and may believe that a notification is late if it is unclear whether it is initial or additional information.

Legislation

Construction (Design and Management) Regulations 1994

● *Regulation 7*

Code of Practice

Managing Health and Safety in Construction (HSG 224: ISBN 0 7176 2139 1)

Guidance

CDM Regulations — Practical Guidance for Planning Supervisors (CIRIA Report 173)

Do exploratory works need to be notified and are they the start of construction works?

Exploratory works will be notifiable if they last 30 days or more, or involve more than 500 person days.

Case Study

A diligent Planning Supervisor forwarded Form F10 to the relevant HSE office eight weeks before the anticipated start-on-site date.

Approximately two weeks before the start on site date, the Planning Supervisor forwarded 'additional information' to the HSE advising of the confirmed start date and number of Contractors.

The Planning Supervisor received a letter from the HSE alleging late notification of the project and possible prosecution should future projects be so notified.

The Planning Supervisor immediately contacted the Principal Inspector of the HSE office to discuss the matter and advised that the initial notification was sent six weeks previously. The Inspector advised that when the receipt of an F10 and the start-on-site date were less than 15 days apart his Department issued a 'standard' advisory warning letter.

The computer was programmed to automatically generate the letter unless the F10 clearly identified that it was 'additional' information.

In this instance, the HSE apologised to the Planning Supervisor and admitted to a clerical error.

Exploratory works usually form part of the main project works and, where they do, it is the total length of the project works that is calculated for notification purposes.

Exploratory works are included in the definition of 'construction works' if they involve the following:

- site clearance
- investigation (but not site survey)
- excavation
- laying and installing the foundations of the structure.

The 'construction phase' of a project commences when the construction works of a project starts.

An exploration works package can be let as a separate contract on a duration of less than 30 days (therefore it will not be notifiable) but which includes *more* than FOUR persons at work at any one time carrying out the construction works. In this instance, the project will come under the requirements of the CDM Regulations and all but Regulation 7 (notification of project) will be applicable.

Site survey works are those which involve taking levels, measurements, setting out and any other visual activities that generally do not involve physical activity, such as drilling bore holes, taking down fixtures, etc.

Legislation

Construction (Design and Management) Regulations 1994

- *Regulation 2*
- *Regulation 3*
- *Regulation 7*

Code of Practice

Managing Health and Safety in Construction (HSG 224: ISBN 0 7176 2139 1)

Is there any recognised qualification which the Planning Supervisor must have?

No. The HSE specifically stated that they did not envisage the CDM Regulations creating a whole new profession of Planning Supervisor.

The Client has to appoint a 'competent' Planning Supervisor and this means someone with the necessary knowledge, experience and ability to carry out the responsibilities set out in the Regulations.

There are numerous courses now available that provide a 'qualification' in Planning Supervisor but such a qualification may not necessarily equate to competency. Did the qualification require an exam to be sat which was independently assessed or was the 'qualification' produced merely on attendance at the course? Would five days of knowledge be sufficient to give a competent understanding of construction methods, design issues, health and safety knowledge?

A formal qualification may be helpful but is not essential when appointing a Planning Supervisor. Useful guidance on what to consider is summarised in Appendix 5.

Legislation

Construction (Design and Management) Regulations 1994
- *Regulation 8*
- *Regulation 9*

Code of Practice

Managing Health and Safety in Construction (HSG 224: ISBN 0 7176 2139 1)

Guidance

A Guide to Managing Health and Safety in Construction (HSE: ISBN 0 7176 07550)

How are the competency and resources of the Planning Supervisor assessed?

A common approach is by way of questionnaire but the answers provided may give only part of the picture. A more pro-active approach would be to seek references from previous Clients and to carry out interviews.

Reasonable enquiries are needed dependent on the size of the project. Finding a Planning Supervisor for a multi-million pound new build will require more extensive checks than appointing one for a refurbishment project, although some small refurbishment projects can be complex and hazardous, requiring knowledge of a wide range of health and safety laws, e.g. Asbestos Regulations, etc.

The Planning Supervisor must be able to demonstrate health and safety knowledge, construction awareness, knowledge of the design process, etc. Information on such issues can be given in writing but could also be obtained by interviewing or obtaining references. The Regulations do not stipulate that enquiries have to be in writing but it would be reasonable to expect some record of how you reached a decision that the Planning Supervisor you appointed was competent and had adequate resources to do the job.

As with many incidents of appointing suitable persons to statutory appointments, engaging the cheapest option may not always be the best decision. Rock bottom fees may mean that resources will not be allocated to the project and you will only get what you pay for, e.g. a phantom Planning Supervisor!

Membership of a professional organisation for Planning Supervisors is *not* a pre-requisite for competency. The HSE did not envisage the creation of a whole new profession and they do not advocate restrictive appointments. However, membership of a professional body, whether dedicated to the function of Planning Supervisor or not, is a good indication of minimum competency levels, continuing professional development commitment and the acceptance of professional conduct standards.

If a questionnaire is used and returned, it is best to have some 'benchmarking' for answers and a scoring assessment can work well. Answers are awarded maximum potential marks and actual answers given are assessed against the ideal. At the end of the questionnaire, a maximum possible score is known and an actual score calculated. If the actual score achieved is less than the 'benchmark' then the applicant has failed your competency test.

See Appendices 6, 7 and 8 for an example of a Planning Supervisor questionnaire, a model answer guide and a questionnaire appraisal form.

Questionnaires may only be part of the process and contact should be made with previous Clients and information should be sought on the performance of the following:

- knowledge of construction processes
- knowledge of health and safety
- evidence of effectiveness to the Design Team
- pragmatic approach
- value for money
- adding value to the project
- continuous improvement initiatives.

Interviews with the organisation (or individual) concerned would also elicit key information.

Legislation

Construction (Design and Management) Regulations 1994

- *Regulation 8*
- *Regulation 9*

Code of Practice

Managing Health and Safety in Construction (HSG 224: ISBN 0 7176 2139 1)

Does the Planning Supervisor have to be independent of the other members of the Design Team?

No. Planning supervision under CDM is a function and not a specific job task. The role can be shared between several disciplines provided they all have competency and resources.

Architects, Quantity Surveyors, Project Managers, Engineers, etc., can all be appointed as Planning Supervisor to a project even if they are already on the Design Team. They may have a separate 'in-house' division who can carry out the function, or specialist health and safety teams.

Independent Planning Supervisors are now common and such an appointment can bring objectivity to a project in respect of health and safety matters. It may be easier for an independent Planning Supervisor to question a Designer's Design Risk Assessment than for the Designer to objectively do it himself. The Planning Supervisor should act as the go-between to all parties — Client and Designer, Client and Principal Contractor, Designer and Contractor, Designer and Designer — and should ensure that there is a good flow of information regarding health and safety of the project.

Legislation

Construction (Design and Management) Regulations 1994

- *Regulation 6*
- *Regulation 8*
- *Regulation 9*

Code of Practice

Managing Health and Safety in Construction (HSG 224: ISBN 0 7176 2139 1)

Guidance

A Guide to Managing Health and Safety in Construction (HSE: ISBN 0 7176 07550)
Designing for Health & Safety in Construction (HSE: ISBN 0 7176 08077)

Can a Client appoint himself as Planning Supervisor?

Yes, provided he can demonstrate that he has the competency and resources to undertake the function.

The Client must be familiar with the requirements of Regulations 14 and 15(i) CDM as these lay down the duties that are applicable to the Planning Supervisor.

The Client must be able to demonstrate knowledge of the construction process, and design function, as well as health and safety knowledge, including fire safety, and be fully conversant with construction practices, etc.

A Client, who is a company, may appoint an employee as Planning Supervisor under the Regulations, e.g. a Facilities Manager or a Project Manager. They must have the resources, including time, to do the job and must not be placed in conflicting situations that are detrimental to the health and safety of the project.

Legislation

Construction (Design and Management) Regulations 1994
- *Regulation 6*
- *Regulation 8*
- *Regulation 9*
- *Regulation 14*
- *Regulation 15*

Code of Practice

Managing Health and Safety in Construction (HSG 224: ISBN 0 7176 2139 1)

Guidance

A Guide to Managing Health and Safety in Construction (HSE: ISBN 0 7176 07550)
Designing for Health & Safety in Construction (HSE: ISBN 0 7176 08077)
CDM Regulations — Practical Guidance for Planning Supervisors (CIRIA Report 173)

Can the Client appoint the Principal Contractor as Planning Supervisor?

Yes, provided the Client is satisfied that the Principal Contractor is competent and has adequate resources to do the job.

If the Principal Contractor has their own health and safety person then they may be in a good position to discharge the duties of Planning Supervisor.

The Planning Supervisor has to have the ability to communicate with the Design Team in order to discuss health and safety issues. A Contractor's Safety Officer could be an ideal person to communicate with the Architect, Building Services Consultant or Structural Engineer because they are familiar with construction processes and could advise the Design Team that the proposed sequence of construction or programming is not the preferred one from a health and safety point of view.

The Principal Contractor must be assessed in the same way that anyone else would be in respect of the position of Planning Supervisor.

Legislation

Construction (Design and Management) Regulations 1994

- *Regulation 6*
- *Regulation 8*
- *Regulation 9*

Code of Practice

Managing Health and Safety in Construction (HSG 224: ISBN 0 7176 2139 1)

Guidance

A Guide to Managing Health and Safety in Construction (HSE: ISBN 0 7176 07550)

How soon does the Planning Supervisor have to be appointed to the project?

As soon as the Client believes that a project is likely to happen, e.g. at feasibility stage or when outline design/planning applications are submitted.

The HSE believe the Planning Supervisor to be a pivotal role in the adoption of health and safety principles throughout the project. They want to ensure that the Planning Supervisor has been involved in the planning stage of the project and that the appointment is not just superficial. The HSE will want to be satisfied that the Planning Supervisor will have had the opportunity to develop the Pre-tender Health and Safety Plan prior to the tendering or negotiating phase of the contract.

The Approved Code of Practice requires the Planning Supervisor to be appointed as soon as is 'practicable' after the Client has such information about the project and the construction work involved.

Legislation

Construction (Design and Management) Regulations 1994

● *Regulation 6*

Code of Practice

Managing Health and Safety in Construction (HSG 224: ISBN 0 7176 2139 1)

Can the Planning Supervisor be changed during the project?

Yes. The Planning Supervisor is a function that is best carried out by people who have the experience and this may vary from stage to stage in a project.

The CDM Regulations allow for the Planning Supervisor to be 'terminated', 'changed' or 'renewed' as necessary to ensure that those appointments remain filled at all times until the end of the construction phase.

The Client must *never* allow a construction project (to which CDM applies) to proceed at any stage without the suitable appointment of a Planning Supervisor.

The Planning Supervisor for the project has to be notified on Form F10 to the HSE as soon as they are appointed. If you choose to change the Planning Supervisor then the *new* Planning Supervisor must notify 'revised information' to the HSE.

A project may start off at the feasibility stage and the Architect or Project Manager may be appointed Planning Supervisor. During the first phase of the project the Planning Supervisor assumes responsibilities for co-ordinating the design, gathering information on the site, e.g. contaminated land surveys, etc., advising the Client and so on. The next phase of the project may be agreed as a Design and Build project. The role of Planning Supervisor could be passed from the Architect or Project Manager to the Design and Build Contractor, provided they can demonstrate competency, as they would be best placed to co-ordinate health and safety issues in the Design and Build phase of the project.

Legislation

Construction (Design and Management) Regulations 1994

● *Regulation 6*

Code of Practice

Managing Health and Safety in Construction (HSG 224: ISBN 0 7176 2139 1)

Does a Client have to take the advice of the Planning Supervisor?

There is nothing in the CDM Regulations that states that the Client must take the advice of the Planning Supervisor. The Planning Supervisor must be in a position to give adequate advice to the Client to enable him to comply with the Regulations concerning competency and resources of Designers and Contractors, and in respect of the adequacy of the Construction Phase Health and Safety Plan, if requested to do so.

If the Planning Supervisor advises the Client that a Designer or Principal Contractor or Contractor is not competent or has inadequate resources and the Client ignores such advice, the HSE would consider the Client to be in serious breach of his duties under CDM Regulations 8 and 9 because 'no person' shall arrange for Designers or Contractors to prepare a design or manage construction works unless reasonably satisfied that they are competent to do so.

Case Study

The Client commissioned a feasibility and concept design project for a new block of residential flats. He appointed an independent Planning Supervisor to the Design Team as he believed that this would provide an objective view to the siting of the flats, access to the site and the overall design, e.g. flat roof versus pitched roof, window cleaning access and so on.

Following receipt of planning permission and lease agreements, the Planning Supervisor drew up an initial Pre-tender Health and Safety Plan dealing with the concept design of the building. The Client's preferred procurement route was 'Design and Build' for the detailed design and construction of the project.

The Planning Supervisor for the concept stage advised the Client that the Design and Build Contractor would be best placed to assume the Planning Supervisor function for the remainder of the project, having satisfied himself on behalf of the Client of the Design and Build Contractor's competency and resources.

The Design and Build Contractor was duly appointed as Planning Supervisor and the HSE was informed by 'revised information' on Form F10.

There is little point in appointing a Planning Supervisor to a project if you do not value their opinion. A Planning Supervisor should have their Client's interest as a priority and should offer advice in respect of the health and safety aspects of the project in an objective and unbiased way.

Should a Client fail to take the advice of his Planning Supervisor he could be in breach of Regulation 7 Management of Health and Safety at Work Regulations 1999 by ignoring the advice of his 'competent' person in relation to health and safety.

Legislation

Construction (Design and Management) Regulations 1994

- *Regulation 8*
- *Regulation 9*
- *Regulation 14*

Management of Health & Safety at Work Regulations 1999

- *Regulation 7*

Code of Practice

Managing Health and Safety in Construction (HSG 224: ISBN 0 7176 2139 1)

Does the Planning Supervisor have to visit the site during the Design Stage?

The role of the Planning Supervisor is to co-ordinate information in respect of health and safety for the project, and to ensure that the Pre-tender Health and Safety Plan is completed.

The Planning Supervisor needs to understand the site, design proposals, hazards and risks of the project, and how all of these things will interrelate to the existing environment.

Planning Supervisors should visit the site to carry out their own survey of health and safety issues and to familiarise themselves with the area, e.g. busy roads, pedestrian flow, access restrictions, etc.

However, there is nothing in the CDM Regulations that requires a Planning Supervisor to visit a site. It could be perfectly acceptable to assimilate vital information for compiling the Health and Safety Plan and for issuing advice on hazards and risks in respect of the project from information supplied by way of surveys, reports, photographs, etc.

An effective Planning Supervisor will always want to visit the site at the beginning of a project and it should be money well spent in allowing them to do so.

Legislation

Construction (Design and Management) Regulations 1994

- *Regulation 11*
- *Regulation 14*

Code of Practice

Managing Health and Safety in Construction (HSG 224: ISBN 0 7176 2139 1)

Does the Planning Supervisor have to carry out site safety inspections once the project has started on site?

No. There is no duty on a Planning Supervisor to undertake any site safety activity in respect of construction works. Therefore you do not need to pay for this service, as it does not need to be carried out under the CDM Regulations.

You may, of course, appoint the Planning Supervisor to carry out this duty for you in addition to their legal responsibilities. It has useful benefits for ensuring that standards of safety are maintained and that the Principal Contractor complies with the Construction Safety Plan. The Planning Supervisor is also in a good position to give advice to the Client after site safety visits. However, site visits during the construction phase do allow the Planning Supervisor to review ongoing design issues and gather information for the Health and Safety File.

If you require the Planning Supervisor to assume the responsibilities of your Safety Adviser, then make sure there is a specific agreement to cover the duties and agree the fee in advance.

Legislation

Construction (Design and Management) Regulations 1994

● *Regulation 14*

Code of Practice

Managing Health and Safety in Construction (HSG 224: ISBN 0 7176 2139 1)

Does the Planning Supervisor have to attend every site meeting?

No. There is no requirement for a Planning Supervisor to do this, as there is no legal duty placed on the Planning Supervisor to be responsible for site safety.

The Planning Supervisor does have a duty to ensure co-operation between Designers so far as is necessary to enable each Designer to comply with the requirements of Regulation 13 CDM, and this may be best achieved by attendance at site meetings so that the Planning Supervisor can ensure health and safety information is freely shared. However, sitting at lengthy site meetings may be an expensive way to achieve this duty when a few regular phone calls can be undertaken to each Designer and the Principal Contractor to ensure that they have all the information they need.

It would be sensible to have the Planning Supervisor attend a site meeting towards the end of the project when they will be able to issue requests for information to all parties for inclusion in the Health and Safety File.

Planning Supervisors may need to attend a specific Design Team meeting if fundamental design changes have been made to the project, as these may have health and safety consequences.

Ensure that your Planning Supervisor is copied in with site meeting minutes and issue instructions to your Planning Supervisor to *read* them and to take whatever appropriate action to ensure they are fully up to speed with the project.

Legislation

Construction (Design and Management) Regulations 1994

● *Regulation 14*

Code of Practice

Managing Health and Safety in Construction (HSG 224: ISBN 0 7176 2139 1)

What fee should be paid for the services of a Planning Supervisor?

Fees can be either on a percentage of project or contract costs or can be a 'fixed fee' for the project.

Percentage costs seem to vary from 0·25% up to 3% depending on project values.

Sometimes a one-off fixed fee and a percentage is charged.

A fixed fee should be based on an hourly or daily rate and the anticipated number of hours/days needed to complete the statutory duties placed on the Planning Supervisor.

Have a clear brief of what you want the Planning Supervisor to do. Base your requirements on the Regulations, i.e. the duties placed on the Planning Supervisor. If you require *other* services, e.g. site safety audits, make sure this is specified as additional services and indicate whether fees are to be included in the percentage or fixed fee or are to be invoiced separately on a time charged basis.

It is easy to pay a lot of money and receive poor value for money when appointing a Planning Supervisor. The position should be beneficial to you and your Design Team and should be a source of advice and information on health and safety issues.

Ask the Planning Supervisor the following questions in order to obtain an indication of how much time they propose to devote to the project:

- How do you intend to gather information regarding the project?
- Will you be carrying out an initial site visit?
- How will you co-ordinate Designer's responsibilities under CDM?
- How do you propose to check Design Risk Assessments?
- How long will it take you to prepare the Pre-tender Health and Safety Plan, submit notification to the HSE, etc.?
- How do you propose to check and thereafter advise me on the adequacy of the Construction Phase Health and Safety Plan?
- How do you propose to advise me on competency and adequacy of resources when I appoint Designers and Contractors? What time have you allowed for this activity?
- How often do you intend to visit the construction site? For what purpose?
- How do you propose to co-ordinate the Mechanical and Electrical Designers and Contractors?
- How will you gather information for the Health and Safety File and how long will it take you to prepare the Health and Safety File?

Legislation

Construction (Design and Management) Regulations 1994

- *Regulation 6*
- *Regulation 7*
- *Regulation 14*

Code of Practice

Managing Health and Safety in Construction (HSG 224: ISBN 0 7176 2139 1)

As Planning Supervisor, my Client wants me to give advice regarding the competency and resources of the Design Team. What do I need to consider?

A Client must not appoint any Designer who is not competent in respect of health and safety matters relating to his design nor must he appoint anyone who does not have the resources to comply with the requirements of Regulation 13.

Many Clients delegate the assessment of the Design Team to their Planning Supervisor. If this is the case, it is important that the Planning Supervisor has a written procedure in place to demonstrate the steps taken.

Step one will be to issue a Designer's questionnaire, which seeks general information about the Designer, partnership, practice or company. Information on the types of projects they normally deal with will be relevant — a design company experienced in domestic dwellings may not necessarily be competent to design industrial buildings.

Details of individual qualifications, membership of professional bodies, etc. will be relevant.

Details of their health and safety policies, procedures and practices will be needed.

Details of how they prepare and consider Design Risk Assessments would be helpful.

Have they had experiences of the type of project before? Ask for references. Go to see similar work. Ask to see examples of Design Risk Assessments.

How do they keep their employees up to date about health and safety issues, design innovations, etc.? Self development through reading is fine but what about their commitment to the subject of health and safety by spending money on courses, etc.

Remember that the Design Team includes:

- Architects
- Quantity Surveyors
- Building Services Consultants
- Structural Engineers
- Civil Engineers
- Project Managers (if they are allowed to *specify*)
- Interior Designers
- Landscape Architects.

All of them should be subjected to competency and resources checks.

Having gathered all relevant information, devise a system where you can quantitatively score their responses to their responsibilities under Regulation 13, i.e. Design Risk Assessments will be very relevant.

Information on any formal or informal action by statutory authorities, e.g. the HSE, will be relevant, as will details of any accidents that have happened to their own personnel or on sites for which they have held some responsibility.

Nominated individuals responsible for health and safety and CDM issues should be included and examples of Safety Policy documents, CDM Procedures and Protocols, etc., should be included with any responses.

Obtaining information is relatively easy. The tricky bit is assessing it objectively so that you can conclude that they are 'competent'. It is easy to believe that all 'professionals' are competent otherwise they would not be in business. Unfortunately, this is not true!

Review the information against a 'benchmark' of acceptable answers. If an answer seems inconsistent or lacks details, request more information.

Just because someone is honest enough to admit to having being served with a Statutory Notice does not mean that they should be excluded automatically. Seek information about what they learned from the experience, what procedures did they review and improve. Persistent contraventions of laws indicate an unwillingness to accept responsibilities and usually implies poor standards and attitudes from management downwards. These Designers would be best avoided.

Approvals can be given for certain types of projects, projects up to 'X' value, etc.

Encourage the Client to develop an 'Approved List' of Designers, which indicates their strengths and weaknesses, approval status, etc. Review the list annually, or more frequently if necessary.

Have they really had experience of your type of project before? Ask for references. Go to see similar work. Ask to see examples of Design Risk Assessments.

Legislation

Construction (Design and Management) Regulations 1994

- *Regulation 8*
- *Regulation 9*
- *Regulation 14*

Code of Practice

Managing Health and Safety in Construction (HSG 224: ISBN 0 7176 2139 1)

Case Study

The Designers' questionnaire, shown in Appendix 9, was issued to all Designers acting on behalf of a major leisure operator, by the Planning Supervisor.

The responses obtained were assessed against a 'Model Answers Benchmark' shown in Appendix 10.

Actual marks were calculated against the total potential marks and all those scoring above 150 were approved.

The Client refuses to accept my advice as Planning Supervisor. What should I do?

The CDM Regulations require the Planning Supervisor to be in a position to give adequate advice to:

- any Client and any Contractor with a view to enabling each of them to comply with the competency and resources requirements of Regulations 8 and 9 in respect of Designers
- any Client with a view to enabling them to comply with the competency and resources requirements of Regulations 8 and 9 in respect of Contractors.

If your advice to the Client is that either Designers or Contractors are not competent or do not have adequate resources in respect of health and safety for the construction project but the Client refuses to accept the advice, it is the *Client* who is in breach of Regulations 8 and 9, as the Client would be 'arranging' for the Designer or Contractor to carry out the design or to carry out or manage the construction work.

The Management of Health & Safety at Work Regulations 1999 requires an employer to appoint a competent person to advise and assist him in undertaking the measures he needs to take to comply with the requirements and prohibitions imposed upon him by or under the relevant statutory provisions. The CDM Regulations were made under the enabling provisions of the Health & Safety at Work Etc. Act 1974 and, therefore, are 'relevant statutory provisions'.

The Planning Supervisor could be classed as a 'competent person' for giving health and safety advice and the Client would be in breach of duty if they failed to consider the advice given.

It is imperative to have written systems in place as a Planning Supervisor which demonstrate what advice has been given to the Client and when.

Provided you have exercised your statutory duties competently as required by CDM, there will be no liability to prosecution because others have failed in their duties.

Legislation

Construction (Design and Management) Regulations 1994

● *Regulation 14*

Management of Health & Safety at Work Regulations 1999

● *Regulation 7*

Code of Practice

Managing Health and Safety in Construction (HSG 224: ISBN 0 7176 2139 1)

The Client wants to pay minimum attention to CDM and to do things on a shoestring. What should I do?

Refuse to accept the commission as Planning Supervisor would be a good starting point. Clients who refuse to accept their legal responsibilities will probably be difficult to work with in other areas and professional integrity is as important as fee income. Even more importantly, a criminal record for failing to discharge the duties of the Planning Supervisor will stay on your records long after the project has finished.

The Client has to allow the Planning Supervisor adequate resources to do the job and has to provide information regarding the construction project. Failure to do so could be a breach of the Client's statutory duties.

The Planning Supervisor role relies heavily on good communication and inter-personal skills because it is largely an 'influencing' role. It would be sensible to discuss with the Client the reasons for his attitude to CDM and why he wishes to avoid his responsibilities. It may be because of fees — a question of what do I get for my money.

A professional approach by the Planning Supervisor would be to explain that there may be no need to appoint a separate, independent Planning Supervisor, and that perhaps another member of the Design Team could fulfil the role, saving on fee expenses.

Advise the Client what in your view needs to be undertaken in order to apply CDM to the project, e.g. what information should be made available and confirm such matters in writing.

Persuade the Client of the benefits of applying CDM, i.e. better planning and design reduces site accidents which, in turn, reduces site delays, etc.

Discuss the type of Health and Safety File that the Client would prefer — perhaps the majority of it could be collected by the Principal Contractor, reducing the time needed by the Planning Supervisor. The Planning Supervisor has to *ensure* that the Health and Safety File is prepared, not actually do the preparation. Likewise with the Pre-tender Health and Safety Plan, the Planning Supervisor does *not* have to prepare it but must *ensure* that it is prepared and issued prior to tendering.

CDM is an approach to planning and managing health and safety on construction sites, and afterwards, when the building is maintained. It should be seen as an integral part of the design and construction process and need not cost considerable sums of money.

Review your own fees! Are you misleading your Client about the complexities of the Planning Supervisor function and demanding fees for unnecessary activities, e.g. site safety visits.

Legislation

Construction (Design and Management) Regulations 1994

- *Regulation 6*
- *Regulation 14*

Code of Practice

Managing Health and Safety in Construction (HSG 224: ISBN 0 7176 2139 1)

Case Study

The Architect acting for a warehouse company contacted a company providing Planning Supervisor services and requested minimum 'CDM input' for a re-roofing project that was programmed for eight weeks. The Principal Contractor had already started works and was to assess the roof by way of ladders only. No notification had been made to the HSE and no Health and Safety Plan had been prepared. The Planning Supervisor advised that over-cladding asbestos cement sheet roofing by drilling holes into the asbestos cement was a very hazardous task, that ladder access was not a 'safe system of work', and that the Client had already breached the CDM Regulations. The Planning Supervisor indicated what should have been done and proposed a reasonable fee to undertake the statutory duties necessary but declined the commission.

The following day the Architect contacted the Planning Supervisor and advised that works had been halted and that the Client wished to appoint the company as Planning Supervisor as a matter of urgency. The project was put back on track within CDM but, more importantly, health and safety issues of asbestos cement and ladder access were addressed to ensure the safety of all operatives.

The Architect would probably have been in breach of their duties by not advising the Client that CDM applied to the project.

5

The Designer

The CDM Regulations place responsibilities on Designers. Who are Designers?

Under the CDM Regulations, Designers are all those who have some input into design issues in respect of a project. These include:

- Architects and Engineers contributing to, or having overall responsibility for, the design
- Building Services Engineers designing details of fixed plant
- Surveyors specifying articles or substances or drawing up specifications for remedial works
- Contractors carrying out design work as part of a Design and Build project
- anyone with authority to specify or to alter the specification of designs to be used for the structure
- Temporary Works Engineers designing formwork and falsework
- Interior Designers, Shopfitters and Landscape Architects.

The above includes Architects, Quantity Surveyors, Structural Engineers, Building Services Engineers, Interior Designers, Project Managers (if they can change or issue specifications), Landscape Architects/Designers, temporary Works Engineers designing propping systems, etc.

The 'Designer' must be carrying on a trade, business or other undertaking in which he prepares a design for a structure. The wording was amended to re-instate the intent of CDM, which had been overturned by a Court case.

Legislation

Construction (Design and Management) Regulations 1994

- *Regulation 2*
- *Regulation 13*

Code of Practice

Managing Health and Safety in Construction (HSG 224: ISBN 0 7176 2139 1)

Guidance

Designing for Health & Safety in Construction (HSE: ISBN 0 7176 08077)

Who decides who is a 'Designer'?

Ultimately, only the Court can make definitive interpretation of the Regulations and determine whether or not an individual or company is liable for the duties imposed on them.

In reality, you must decide yourself whether or not you fall within the definition given in Regulation 2 CDM, as amended. The new wording of Regulation 2 reads as follows:

> designer means any person who carries on a trade, business or undertaking in connection with which he prepares a design relating to a structure or part of a structure.

The Client can decide that he expects all his Design Team to assume 'Designer responsibilities' and may conduct competency and resources assessments on all members of the Design Team. By doing this, the Client will be able to show that he took steps to show that he was 'reasonably satisfied' in regarding the Designer's competency and resources.

It would be prudent to discuss with any professional indemnity insurers their definition of 'Designer' under CDM and to ensure that you have appropriate insurance cover for the role you carry out.

Legislation

Construction (Design and Management) Regulations 1994

- *Regulation 2*
- *Regulation 13*

Code of Practice

Managing Health and Safety in Construction (HSG 224: ISBN 0 7176 2139 1)

Guidance

Designing for Health & Safety in Construction (HSE: ISBN 0 7176 08077)

What are the responsibilities of a Designer?

Designers from all disciplines have a contribution to make in avoiding and reducing health and safety risks which are inherent in the construction process and subsequent work, e.g. maintenance.

The most important contribution a Designer can make to improve health and safety will often be at the concept and feasibility stage where various options can be considered so as to avoid potential health and safety issues.

Designers must therefore give due regard to health and safety in their design work.

Designers must provide adequate information about health and safety risks of the design to those who need it, e.g. proposed roof access routes, use of fragile materials, etc.

Designers must co-operate with the Planning Supervisor and other Designers on the project and ensure that information is freely available regarding health and safety issues and that they consider the implications of their designs with other aspects of the design, e.g. structural works in relation to building services, etc.

Designers must advise Clients of their duties under CDM, as specified in Regulation 13 (1). CDM requires Designers to take reasonable steps to advise their Clients of the existence of CDM, their duties within the Regualtions, the existence of the Approved Code of Practice, good health and safety management, and the benefit of making early appointments.

Legislation

Construction (Design and Management) Regulations 1994

● *Regulation 13*

Code of Practice

Managing Health and Safety in Construction (HSG 224: ISBN 0 7176 2139 1)

Guidance

Designing for Health & Safety in Construction (HSE: ISBN 0 7176 08077)

The Planning Supervisor keeps asking for 'Design Risk Assessments'. What are these?

Design Risk Assessment is the technical term given to the formal consideration of health and safety issues relevant to your design.

As a Designer, you should understand that the term 'Hierarchy of Risk Control' is a step by step process of eliminating, minimising or controlling health and safety hazards and risks.

Step 1: Eliminate the hazard and risk.
Step 2: Minimise the hazard and reduce the risk.
Step 3: Control the hazard and risk at source.
Step 4: Control the hazard and risk within the workplace.

In simple terms:

Step 1: Do not design something which could cause injury or ill-health.
Step 2: If you have to continue with the design, ensure you include safety features.
Step 3: Provide safety features etc. at the site of the hazard.
Step 4: Ensure that everyone is issued with personal protective equipment.

Design Risk Assessments set out how you have considered the health and safety aspects of your design and record your decisions.

The first rule of health and safety is to eliminate hazard and risk. If this is not possible, do the next best thing by designing in safety features or specifying different material, etc.

Design Risk Assessments do not have to be detailed or complicated forms that cover everyday situations. They need to be specific to the project and should highlight *unusual* design considerations.

Designers should consider not only *how* the structure will be built and identify these hazards and risks, but must also consider how the building will be used in the future for maintenance and cleaning purposes as well as how it will be occupied.

The considerations you have made in respect of health and safety can be included in your drawings, provided the information is clear and unambiguous.

Each project could have a simple Design Risk Assessment sheet attached to the Project File, indicating how you made the key health and safety decisions. An example of a Design Risk Assessment Form is shown in Appendix 11.

Legislation

Construction (Design and Management) Regulations 1994

● *Regulation 13*

Code of Practice

Managing Health and Safety in Construction (HSG 224: ISBN 0 7176 2139 1)

Guidance

Designing for Health & Safety in Construction (HSE: ISBN 0 7176 08077)
CDM Regulations — Work Sector Guidance for Designers (CIRIA Report 166)
CDM Regulations — Case Studies for Designers (CIRIA Report 145)
Information on Site Safety for Designers of Small Building Projects (HSE Research Report 72/1995)

Are Designers permitted to specify fragile materials?

Fragile materials, i.e. materials that give way on impact, point loading, etc., are a major cause of both construction accidents and building maintenance accidents. Many of these accidents end as fatalities, or with disabling injuries.

Fragile materials constitute a safety hazard and a Design Risk Assessment must be completed that outlines the consideration given in the design process to the use of fragile material, substitute options, etc.

The risks associated with fragile materials are falling through them, injury, death, collapse, causing injury to those below, etc.

As the first responsibility of a Designer is to *eliminate* known hazards, the implication is that fragile materials should not be designed or specified into a project.

If the design scheme demands, for example, a glazed atrium roof, then there are inherent hazards with the design. A solid non-fragile material cannot be specified because the glazing is needed to allow for natural lighting. Where such a scenario exists, the Designer must specify safety features for the glazed atrium, e.g. safety railings, guard rails, running rail and safety harness fittings, gantry access, etc., and also reduce the risk with the use of safety glass.

A netting could be designed underneath the glazed atrium to prevent falls should the material should give way. Access for cleaning of the glazing, maintenance of the paintwork of the frame, etc., need to be considered during the design.

If fragile material is used and design considerations allow a *residual* risk, then the Designer must specify information which must be included in the Health and Safety File. The Designer may recommend that a 'Permit to Work/Enter' system is adopted by the premises occupier, and that additional safety precautions are needed. The Designer must also consider the safety precautions which the Principal Contractor should adopt so as to ensure safe erection or construction of the fragile material.

Legislation

Construction (Design and Management) Regulations 1994

● *Regulation 13*

Code of Practice

Managing Health and Safety in Construction (HSG 224: ISBN 0 7176 2139 1)

Guidance

A Guide to Managing Health and Safety in Construction (HSE: ISBN 0 7176 07550)

Designing for Health & Safety in Construction (HSE: ISBN 0 7176 08077)

Information on Site Safety for Designers of Small Building Projects (HSE 1995)

CDM Regulations — Work Sector Guidance for Designers (CIRIA 1997)

CDM Regulations — Case Studies for Designers (CIRIA 1995)

Can the Planning Supervisor require changes to designs?

No, unless the Client has included this duty as a specific requirement in their agreement with the Planning Supervisor.

However, the Planning Supervisor has to ensure that Designers have had adequate regard to their responsibilities for considering health and safety during the project design process, and where they believe the Designer has been reticent they are duty bound to raise their concerns with the Designer.

The Planning Supervisor should be an expert source of advice about applying the Hierarchy of Risk Control and, whenever necessary, should be consulted by the Designers.

The Planning Supervisor must use best endeavours to advise the Designer if they have concerns about safety issues and must look for alternatives, compromises, etc. If the Designer refuses to listen, then the Planning Supervisor will need to advise the Client of a potential conflict, particularly if the Planning Supervisor believes there will be implications for future occupancy, e.g. specifying fragile roof coverings unnecessarily.

If the Designer refuses to listen to advice offered by the Planning Supervisor regarding health and safety in design issues, then the Designer may be in a vulnerable position should future accidents occur as a result of the design principles chosen.

Prosecution of the Designer will be possible under Regulation 13 CDM and the prosecution case would be strengthened if evidence were available that the Designer refused to listen to professional advice.

If the Planning Supervisor's advice is ignored, it may provide the Planning Supervisor with sufficient evidence to question the competency of the Designer under Regulation 8 and they may advise the Client accordingly, leading to the Designer being dismissed from any approved list, or indeed from the project.

Legislation

Construction (Design and Management) Regulations 1994

● *Regulation 14*

Code of Practice

Managing Health and Safety in Construction (HSG 224: ISBN 0 7176 2139 1)

Guidance

Designing for Health & Safety in Construction (HSE: ISBN 0 7176 08077)

What can Designers be prosecuted for under the CDM Regulations?

Any Designer can be prosecuted for not complying with their statutory duties.

If you fail to advise your Client about their duties under CDM you can be prosecuted. If you *do* advise your Client about the requirement to apply CDM to a project and they ignore your advice, provided you have written records that you did everything reasonably practicable to advise and inform your Client of their duties, you may have a defence against prosecution, the HSE preferring to bring the prosecution against the Client.

However, you will need to consider carefully whether you should be working for a Client whom you know to be blatantly ignoring the law. Professional ethics may preclude such an appointment.

If your Client has not appointed a Planning Supervisor nor a Principal Contractor, nor provides information, then you will have great difficulty in carrying out your own statutory CDM duties.

You can also be prosecuted for failing to comply with your duties to design any construction works safely and with a view to foreseeable risks.

If an accident were to happen on site and the subsequent investigation by the HSE concluded that you, as a Designer, had specified a not commonly known fragile material as a roof covering and that you had not given any information on the hazardous nature of the material to the Planning Supervisor or Principal Contractor, then it could be argued that the accident was due to your negligence because you had failed to specify safety precautions or had failed to supply relevant information to allow others to specify safety precautions to be taken.

If, as a Designer, you are insistent on specifying heavy weight blocks or materials for use on the project, and adequate provision has not been made for handling them on site, e.g. the provision of mechanical aids, then you could be liable for any accident or claims.

Equally, you could be liable to a prosecution if you specify a substance which is severely harmful, i.e. causes cancer, when there are suitable alternatives on the market.

Legislation

Construction (Design and Management) Regulations 1994

- *Regulation 13*

Code of Practice

Managing Health and Safety in Construction (HSG 224: ISBN 0 7176 2139 1)

Guidance

Designing for Health & Safety in Construction (HSE: ISBN 0 7176 08077)

Are the CDM Regulations designed to stifle all design creativity?

No. The Regulations impose, for the first time, responsibilities on Designers to consider health and safety issues in respect of their designs.

Many accidents happen on construction sites because Designers give no consideration to the materials they specify, the buildability process, and the time and resources it takes to do the job. Research by the European Community found that Designers can have a tremendous influence over the number of site accidents and industry ill-health by giving more thought to health and safety in their design.

The CDM Regulations do not intend to bring all building design into uniform grey boxes but expect buildings with design flair to be safe to build and safe for future use.

Designers can still do adventurous things but must consider the practicalities and safety of their designs. Glazed atriums are ideal for some buildings and are perfectly acceptable provided consideration is given to safety issues, such as:

- protection from falling through the fragile material
- access for cleaning
- access for maintenance
- lighting features.

Provided solutions are given and that the design incorporates these, there is nothing legally that can prevent a Designer designing a glazed atrium.

Buildings can be innovative in design but they need to be practical and safe for all future occupiers. Consider the 'Hierarchy of Risk Control' for all design intentions and you will comply with the law.

Case Study

A firm of Architects was prosecuted by the HSE for failing to inform their Client of their duties under CDM Regulations. They allowed a project, to which CDM applied, to progress through the design phase and construction phase without the appointment of a Planning Supervisor or Principal Contractor. The Client was not aware that the two appointments were necessary. In addition, there was no Construction Phase Health and Safety Plan for approval by the Client, causing the Client to have breached Regulation 10 CDM (although they were not prosecuted). The Architects were fined £300 but, more importantly, they have gained a criminal record.

Legislation

Construction (Design and Management) Regulations 1994

• *Regulation 13*

Code of Practice

Managing Health and Safety in Construction (HSG 224: ISBN 0 7176 2139 1)

Guidance

Designing for Health & Safety in Construction (HSE: ISBN 0 7176 08077)
CDM Regulations — Work Sector Guidance for Designers (CIRIA Report 166)

Do duties as a Designer under the CDM Regulations only apply when the project is notifiable?

No. Your duties as a Designer under Regulation 13 CDM apply to all projects where there is design. There does not have to be a Client, Planning Supervisor or Principal Contractor.

Therefore, for all design commissions you must have a procedure in place for documenting how you comply with the legal responsibilities imposed on Designers.

Legislation

Construction (Design and Management) Regulations 1994

• *Regulation 13*

Case Study

Designers of a new concept retailing outlet sourced a unique mesh type ceiling material which was to be installed in one single sheet to give a ripple effect to the ceiling.

Design considerations included the following.

- How is it delivered to site?
- Will it be difficult to handle?
- Will the metal mesh have jagged edges?
- How will it be fixed to the ceiling frame?
- How will lighting be fixed?
- How will sprinklers be fixed?
- Will it be a fragile surface?
- How could maintenance personnel walk above it to access fittings?
- How will it be cleaned?

All of the above, and many more, formed part of the Design Risk Assessment. The Planning Supervisor was asked to comment on the information available and to offer any advice.

The new ceiling concept was installed and created the innovative design which the Designers and Client had wanted.

Code of Practice

Managing Health and Safety in Construction (HSG 224: ISBN 0 7176 2139 1)

Guidance

Designing for Health & Safety in Construction (HSE: ISBN 0 7176 08077)

Can the health and safety considerations of designs be left to the Planning Supervisor?

No. The legal duty to consider health and safety matters in design rests with *Designers.*

The Planning Supervisor can be used for advice on how to apply the Hierarchy of Risk Control and may have experiences of what has worked in similar design scenarios.

You must provide information to the Planning Supervisor when asked to do so. The Planning Supervisor has to ensure that Designers co-operate with each other — sharing information which could have health and safety implications.

The Planning Supervisor must ensure that the Designer includes adequate regard for health and safety issues among the design considerations and, therefore, has a duty to ask relevant questions to establish that this has been the case. Therefore, you must expect the Planning Supervisor to want to see your Design Risk Assessments and to discuss them with you, making recommendations if appropriate.

Legislation

Construction (Design and Management) Regulations 1994

● *Regulation 13*

Code of Practice

Managing Health and Safety in Construction (HSG 224: ISBN 0 7176 2139 1)

Guidance

Designing for Health & Safety in Construction (HSE: ISBN 0 7176 08077)

As Designer, I advise the Client of their responsibilities under the CDM Regualtions and yet they refuse to make any of the statutory appointments or address the Regulations. Am I liable to be prosecuted if the project goes ahead?

No. Provided you have fulfilled your responsibility to advise the Client about the CDM Regulations and how, in your opinion, they will be applicable to the project, you will not be liable to a prosecution (unless of course you fail in any other duties imposed on Designers under the Regulations).

It would be advisable to have a system of written notification to a Client that CDM applies to the project. This would demonstrate that you had taken your responsibilities seriously.

A Client who was properly briefed about CDM by the Designer, but who refused to appoint a Planning Supervisor or Principal Contractor for the project, or made the appointment too late, will be in breach of the Regulations and will be liable to prosecution by the HSE.

Legislation

Construction (Design and Management) Regulations 1994

- *Regulation 6*
- *Regulation 13*

Code of Practice

Managing Health and Safety in Construction (HSG 224: ISBN 0 7176 2139 1)

6

The Principal Contractor

What is, and what are the duties of, the Principal Contractor under the CDM Regulations?

The Principal Contractor is a legal appointment which the Client has to make under the CDM Regulations.

The Principal Contractor must be a Contractor, i.e. someone who either undertakes or manages construction work. A Client who normally co-ordinates construction works carried out on their premises, and who is competent and adequately resourced, can be a Principal Contractor.

The Principal Contractor would normally be a person carrying out or managing the construction work on the project to which they are appointed, i.e. the main or managing Contractor. However, where specialist work is involved, it may be appropriate to appoint the specialist Contractor as Principal Contractor as they would be more suited to managing the risks of the specialist activity.

The Principal Contractor has specific duties under the CDM Regulations and, ultimately, carries responsibility for site safety issues.

The main duties can be summed up as follows.

- Develop and implement the Construction Phase Health and Safety Plan.
- Appoint only competent and properly resourced Contractors to the project, e.g. specialist Contractors and Sub-contractors.
- Obtain and check Method Statements from Contractors.
- Ensure the co-operation and co-ordination of Contractors while they are on site, i.e. control multi-occupied site working.

- Ensure health and safety training is carried out.
- Develop appropriate communication arrangements between Contractors in respect of site health and safety issues.
- Make arrangements for discussing health and safety issues relative to the project.
- Allow only authorised persons onto the site.
- Display Form F10 on site for all operatives to be able to see the details.
- Monitor health and safety performance on site.
- Pass information to the Planning Supervisor for the Health and Safety File.

The Principal Contractor is a critical appointment to the construction project as the standard of site safety will be determined by the commitment and competency of the appointment.

Legislation

Construction (Design and Management) Regulations 1994

- *Regulation 6*
- *Regulation 15*
- *Regulation 16*
- *Regulation 17*
- *Regulation 18*

Code of Practice

Managing Health and Safety in Construction (HSG 224: ISBN 0 7176 2139 1)

Guidance

A Guide to Managing Health and Safety in Construction (HSE: ISBN 0 7176 07550)

When is the Principal Contractor appointed and how is this done?

The Client has to appoint the Principal Contractor as soon as is practicable after having acquired information about the construction aspects of the project, and in good time so that the Client can determine the competency and resources of the Principal Contractor.

If the preferred Contractor is known prior to the tendering or negotiating phase of the project, he should be appointed early in the design process.

Usually, the Principal Contractor is appointed as a result of the tendering process and is usually the successful tenderer.

The appointment of a Principal Contractor is often assumed, or is a verbal instruction, but it is best defined in writing from either the Client, Contract Administrator or Planning Supervisor (if requested to do so).

The Preliminaries in the Bill of Quantities may stipulate that the successful tenderer will be appointed Principal Contractor. Equally, a statement can be made in the Pre-tender Health and Safety Plan.

The timing of the appointment should allow the Principal Contractor opportunity to develop the Construction Phase Health and Safety Plan.

Legislation

Construction (Design and Management) Regulations 1994

- *Regulation 6*

Code of Practice

Managing Health and Safety in Construction (HSG 224: ISBN 0 7176 2139 1)

Can anyone be appointed as Principal Contractor?

No. You must appoint only competent persons who normally carry out the business of a Contractor.

A Contractor is defined in Regulation 2 of CDM as:

Any person who carries on a trade, business or other undertaking (whether for profit or not) in connection with which he:
(a) undertakes to or does carry out or manage construction works,
(b) arranges for any person at work under his control (including where he is an employer, any employee of his) to carry out or manage construction work.

The traditional 'Main' Contractor could be appointed Principal Contractor, as could a Design and Build Contractor, Management Contractor, or Construction Project Manager. If a nominated Sub-contractor or specialist Contractor has more health and safety experience than the Main Contractor they could be appointed Principal Contractor.

A Principal Contractor does *not* have to be the biggest or Main Contractor on the site but whoever is Principal Contractor must be able to influence and control site safety throughout the project.

Legislation

Construction (Design and Management) Regulations 1994

- *Regulation 2*
- *Regulation 6*

Code of Practice

Managing Health and Safety in Construction (HSG 224: ISBN 0 7176 2139 1)

Guidance

A Guide to Managing Health and Safety in Construction (HSE: ISBN 0 7176 07550)

Can a Client appoint himself as Principal Contractor?

A Principal Contractor must be a 'Contractor', i.e. someone who carries on a trade, business or other undertaking in connection with which they:

- undertake to, or do carry out or manage, construction work
- arrange for any person at work under his control (including where he is an employer, any employee of his) to carry out or manage construction work.

If the Client has an in-house Project Management Team who will be supervising and managing the construction work, and provided they are competent and have the resources to do so, they could appoint themselves Principal Contractor.

In-house maintenance and facilities management departments could appoint themselves as Principal Contractor if they undertake the works themselves, or if they are managing the construction process.

The complexity of the construction project has to be considered and appointments made only within core competencies, e.g. facilities or maintenance teams may not be competent to manage the health and safety of a new-build office complex or an industrial unit constructed with a portal frame.

A Client who appoints the Office Manager as Principal Contractor in respect of a new office extension would be likely to be contravening the Regulations because the Office Manager would not normally carry out or manage construction works — he would not be a Contractor and, certainly, is unlikely to be competent.

Legislation

Construction (Design and Management) Regulations 1994

- *Regulation 6*
- *Regulation 8*
- *Regulation 9*

Code of Practice

Managing Health and Safety in Construction (HSG 224: ISBN 0 7176 2139 1)

What does the Principal Contractor have to do and, as the Client, will I have to pay additional fees?

The Principal Contractor is responsible for site safety, assessing competency and resources of Contractors, co-ordinating work activities, organising site training, setting-up communication between Contractors, and monitoring site safety.

The Principal Contractor must develop the Pre-tender Health and Safety Plan into the *Construction* Phase Health and Safety Plan. This plan is a critical document that sets out the rules for safety on site, how the site will be managed, arrangements for training and communication, welfare facilities, etc.

In addition, the Principal Contractor must appoint competent Contractors, carry out induction training, provide protective equipment for general use, carry out general Risk Assessments and co-ordinate the health and safety of all trades working on the project.

The Principal Contractor's duties involve co-ordinating and planning site safety. Therefore it takes time and resources and these must be paid for. If the project is tendered on a Bill of Quantities or is negotiated, then an allowance should be included for undertaking the role of Principal Contractor.

The costs will depend on the value and duration of the project.

You must, as Client, allow your Principal Contractor resources to do the job. This means ensuring that adequate financial provision is made to do the job properly. You may need to allow for a full-time Safety Manager on site — this should be included in the Pre-tender Health and Safety Plan (if appropriate) and an item should be included in the Preliminaries for costing purposes.

If the Principal Contractor is effective at managing, co-ordinating, planning and monitoring site safety, it should have beneficial effects on the project in both financial and time-scale terms. Good site organisation could reduce site accidents and downtime, thereby allowing the project to progress in accordance with the construction programme.

Poorly managed sites create 'accidents waiting to happen'. Accidents cost all parties money to a greater or lesser extent, including the Client. Therefore, additional fees in the 'prelims' may be recouped many times over by having fewer accidents or near misses on site.

Legislation

Construction (Design and Management) Regulations 1994

- *Regulation 15*
- *Regulation 16*
- *Regulation 17*
- *Regulation 18*

Code of Practice

Managing Health and Safety in Construction (HSG 224: ISBN 0 7176 2139 1)

Guidance

A Guide to Managing Health and Safety in Construction (HSE: ISBN 0 7176 07550)

Case Study

A large retail building project contained a requirement in the Pre-tender Health and Safety Plan for a full-time Safety Manager to be appointed to the project. The tendering Contractors proposed to cover site health and safety responsibilities by using visiting Health and Safety Consultants every two weeks. This was not considered appropriate resources by the Planning Supervisor who was advising the Client and, in order to secure the Tender, the preferred Contractor had to agree to appoint a full-time Health and Safety Manager for the duration of the project. Costs were allowed to cover the appointment.

On the same project, the Pre-tender Health and Safety Plan and Preliminaries in the Bill of Quantities required the Principal Contractor to guard all openings over two metres within the site.

A cost was allowed to provide guard rails, etc., and the Principal Contractor was happy to provide everything necessary as he had 'priced for the job'.

Part 3

Proceeding to site

Chapter summary

Chapter 7 The Client

Covers Client duties as the project gets ready to start on site, e.g. assessing the Construction Phase Health and Safety Plan, and providing information.

Chapter 8 The Planning Supervisor

Deals with questions on the key duties of the role before works start on site.

Chapter 9 The Designer

Questions review the Designer's role in providing information, key duties, hazards and risks of design.

Chapter 10 The Principal Contractor

A key role for the Principal Contractor is in the run up to starting on site. This chapter looks at the appointment of the Principal Contractor and issues relating to it.

Chapter 11 The Pre-tender Health and Safety Plan

Questions and answers on what the document is, who prepares it, what it has to contain, who should have copies, etc.

Chapter 12 The Construction Phase Health and Safety Plan

What is it, who compiles it, and who needs to have a copy of it? Fire safety plans, other health and safety legislation applicable to construction sites are some of the issues covered in this chapter.

7

The Client

What are the duties of a Client before giving the go ahead for a construction project to start on site?

You must ensure that you have complied with the CDM requirements to appoint *competent* Designers, Planning Supervisor and Principal Contractor. Each of these functions must also have adequate resources to carry out the tasks required.

An assessment of competency and resources needs to have been carried out and this process should be ongoing throughout the duration of the project, although the Client has no legal duty to monitor the standards of his appointees during the project.

The only specific legal duty on the Client prior to construction work commencing is to ensure that the Construction Phase Health and Safety Plan has been prepared.

The Client does *not* have to approve it but must ensure that it complies with Regulation 15 (4), and that it is 'suitable and sufficient'.

If necessary, the Client can ask the Planning Supervisor for advice on the suitability of the Plan.

The Client has an implied duty to ensure that the Principal Contractor has sufficient *time* to prepare the Construction Phase Health and Safety Plan prior to the commencement of works.

Legislation

Construction (Design and Management) Regulations 1994

- *Regulation 8*
- *Regulation 9*
- *Regulation 10*

Code of Practice

Managing Health and Safety in Construction (HSG 224: ISBN 0 7176 2139 1)

As Client, I have changed my mind about the design before starting on site. What should I do?

The Design Team is responsible for ensuring that the Client is kept informed of CDM responsibilities and they must advise you that they will need to reconsider your new design and produce new Design Risk Assessments. These Design Risk Assessments will need to be handed to the Planning Supervisor so that he can ensure that key information of health and safety hazards and risks is passed to the Principal Contractor. In turn, the Principal Contractor must ensure that he addresses the design risks within the Construction Phase Health and Safety Plan.

Again, the Principal Contractor may need time to alter the Plan and make additional safety arrangements so, as Client, you must ensure that you give the Principal Contractor adequate time to comply with the Regulations. Delaying the date when construction work is intended to start will be almost unavoidable.

Legislation

Construction (Design and Management) Regulations 1994

- *Regulation 8*
- *Regulation 9*
- *Regulation 13*
- *Regulation 15*

Guidance

Managing Health and Safety in Construction (HSG 224: ISBN 0 7176 2139 1)

When must the Client appoint a Principal Contractor?

A Client must appoint a Principal Contractor as soon as is practicable after the Client has such information about the project and the construction work involved in it as will enable the Client to comply with the requirements to assess the competency and resources of any Contractor appointed to carry out or manage construction works.

It is essential that the Principal Contractor is appointed in sufficient time to develop the Health and Safety Plan before construction works start.

If a contract is to be negotiated with a preferred Contractor, it is essential that they are formally advised that they are deemed to be Principal Contractor for the project under CDM Regulations. A formal letter of appointment would be sensible. An example is shown in Appendix 12.

If a construction contract is to be awarded by competitive tender, it would be useful to include an introductory paragraph in the Pre-tender Health and Safety Plan, which is sent to all tenderers, that states that the successful tenderer for the project will be deemed to be Principal Contractor as defined in the CDM Regulations.

Information and/or clarification on who will be appointed Principal Contractor can be included in the Bill of Quantities or Employers' Requirements.

Legislation

Construction (Design and Management) Regulations 1994

● *Regulation 6*

Code of Practice

Managing Health and Safety in Construction (HSG 224: ISBN 0 7176 2139 1)

Guidance

A Guide to Managing Health and Safety in Construction (HSE: ISBN 0 7176 07550)

As Client, how do I assess the adequacy of the Construction Phase Health and Safety Plan?

The Client cannot allow construction works to commence without a Health and Safety Plan having been prepared which complies with Regulation 15 (4).

Often the Client requires the Planning Supervisor to advise on the suitability of the Construction Health and Safety Plan, indeed the Planning Supervisor legally has to be in a position to give adequate advice.

The Construction Phase Health and Safety Plan should be a practical document which is site specific. That means it must address health and safety issues relevant to the development project and the actual site conditions.

It is sensible to have a checklist of requirements which the Health and Safety Plan must meet and to compare the information given in the Plan to 'model answers'.

The Health and Safety Plan must be compiled by the Principal Contractor prior to commencement of construction works and it will help them if you were to require the Planning Supervisor to issue a guide as to how you expect the Construction Phase Plan to be laid out and what information you expect it to contain.

An example of a pro-forma Construction Phase Health and Safety Plan is shown in Appendix 13.

The critical question is whether the Plan is site specific, i.e. does it include information about this particular project in respect of:

- management of health and safety on the site and who is responsible for what
- risks involved in the construction works on *this* project
- any activities that need to be undertaken on the site by any person which could affect the health, safety and welfare of others at work on the site, or resorting to the site
- welfare arrangements for the site
- monitoring and reviewing health and safety issues on the site.

It is not necessary for a Construction Phase Safety Plan to be approximately two inches thick and to include every Method Statement under the sun.

It is more important that everyone on the site knows who is who, who will undertake Risk Assessments, who will organise and inspect communal access equipment, e.g. scaffolding, what training is to be provided, etc.

The Construction Phase Health and Safety Plan does not have to be totally complete before works start on site. It must include as much information as possible, particularly about site set-up procedures, initial enabling or stripping out works. The Plan needs to be developed as works progress — it is a 'dynamic' document which should be updated as works progress on site.

Not all of the design issues may have been decided and Designers' Risk Assessments may be produced during the project. These need to be interpreted by the Principal Contractor and incorporated into the Construction Phase Health and Safety Plan. Therefore, the document can never be totally complete on day one.

A checklist which can be used to assess a Construction Phase Health and Safety Plan is shown in Appendix 14.

When you have assessed the Plan, confirm in writing whether you find it acceptable or not and confirm to the Project Architect (and other Design Team members) and the Principal Contractor whether works can commence on site.

An example of a Construction Phase Health and Safety Plan Assessment Notice is shown in Appendix 15.

Legislation

Construction (Design and Management) Regulations 1994

- *Regulation 14*
- *Regulation 15*

Code of Practice

Managing Health and Safety in Construction (HSG 224: ISBN 0 7176 2139 1)

Case Study

An HSE Inspector visited a site where asbestos boarding was being removed. He reviewed the Construction Phase Health and Safety Plan and determined that it was not adequate in so far as it did not comply with Regulation 15 (4). It was too general and not site specific.

The Inspector served a Prohibition Notice on the Principal Contractor, prohibiting the carrying out of any construction works on the site until a suitable Health and Safety Plan had been produced, complying with Regulation 15 (4).

All works of construction had to cease immediately on receipt of the Prohibition Notice and could not re-commence until the Inspector had approved the Plan and withdrawn the Prohibition Notice.

8

The Planning Supervisor

What key duties should the Planning Supervisor have completed before a project starts on site?

The majority of the Planning Supervisor's duties are undertaken before works commence on site.

The Planning Supervisor has to ensure the following.

- All parties who carry out design work on a project collaborate with each other and pay attention to reducing risks to health and safety wherever possible.
- The design is being progressed to avoid foreseeable risks, or where this is not possible, to combat risks at source.
- All Designers co-operate with each other and provide information to each other in order that health and safety risks can be assessed.
- A Pre-tender Health and Safety Plan has been produced and that it has been developed into the Construction Phase Health and Safety Plan prior to commencement of construction works.
- Advice has been given to the Client if requested, in respect of the suitability of the Construction Phase Health and Safety Plan.
- Advice has been given to the Client on the competency and resources of the Designers and Principal Contractor.
- That Form F10 has been sent to the HSE, having been updated with additional information, as necessary.

The Planning Supervisor should have a major influence over the Design Team in respect of considering health and safety issues from the design and the construction methods envisaged for the construction phase.

The role of co-ordinating the Design Team is an important one for the Planning Supervisor as it means that all the different Designers, e.g. Architects, Interior Designers, Building Services Consultants, Quantity Surveyors, etc., should interact with one another to ensure that each of their respective designs do not conflict or create foreseeable health and safety risks.

Legislation

Construction (Design and Management) Regulations 1994

● *Regulation 14*

Code of Practice

Managing Health and Safety in Construction (HSG 224: ISBN 0 7176 2139 1)

Do the CDM Regulations apply to Mechanical and Electrical Contractors?

Mechanical and Electrical Contractors can be Designers under the Regulations if they design, i.e. draw, issue design details, issue specifications or Bills of Quantities.

If so, Regulation 13 applies to them and they must produce Design Risk Assessments. As Planning Supervisor you must ensure that these Design Risk Assessments are shared with the other Designers, highlighting for them any key hazards that they may need to be aware of, e.g. the Mechanical and Electrical Contractor has designed for a ten tonne piece of mechanical plant to be located on the flat roof. The Architect will need to know so that he can plan for edge protection or safe access routes. The Structural Engineer will need to know so that he can determine whether the roof will take the load, etc. The Principal Contractor will need to know because he will be responsible for organising cranage to lift the plant into place.

If Mechanical and Electrical Contractors have *no* design responsibility, they are then Contractors who come under the responsibility of the Principal Contractor. They must produce whatever health and safety information the Principal Contractor requires, e.g. Method Statements, Risk Assessments, etc.

There is no reason why a Mechanical and Electrical Contractor cannot be appointed as Principal Contractor on a project, provided they can demonstrate competency and resources.

Legislation

Construction (Design and Management) Regulations 1994

- *Regulation 2*
- *Regulation 13*
- *Regulation 14*

Code of Practice

Managing Health and Safety in Construction (HSG 224: ISBN 0 7176 2139 1)

Guidance

A Guide to Managing Health and Safety in Construction (HSE: ISBN 0 7176 07550)
CDM Regulations — Practical Guidance for Planning Supervisors (CIRIA Report 173)

9

The Designer

What are a Designer's key responsibilities before a construction project commences on site?

The duties of Designers are itemised in Regulation 13. The predominant duty of a Designer is to manage the process of hazard and risk in respect of health and safety, as a Designer has responsibility to reduce hazards within his designs and also in respect of materials, methods and processes that he specifies for the construction phase.

Designers must consider the consequences of their designs in relation to future maintenance and cleaning.

All aspects of hazard and risk in relation to the design must have been considered before works commence on site.

The acceptable way to consider hazards and risks is to produce Design Risk Assessments. These should have been produced before construction commencement and passed to the Planning Supervisor for inclusion in the Pre-tender Health and Safety Plan.

The principles of Regulation 13 (2) must be followed in respect of risk assessments, namely:

- eliminate the hazards
- tackle hazards at source by designs which reduce the risks to an acceptable level
- develop designs that protect all people exposed to the hazard and not rely on control measures which just protect an individual.

Legislation

Construction (Design and Management) Regulations 1994

● *Regulation 13*

Code of Practice

Managing Health and Safety in Construction (HSG 224: ISBN 0 7176 2139 1)

Is there a recognised format for Design Risk Assessments?

No. The CDM Regulations do not specify an exact format that has to be used for Design Risk Assessments. They require merely that hazards and risks in the design are considered and, where appropriate, recorded so that the information can be passed to other members of the Design Team, the Planning Supervisor and all contractors, as appropriate.

Suitable information on hazards and risks can be annotated on drawings if this will give clear guidance to whoever will be reading the drawings. Information can equally be collated in pro-forma Design Risk Assessment forms — see Appendix 11 for an example.

If drawings are designed on computer-aided design systems, text can be annotated to drawings to convey hazard and risks and the proposed control measures.

Information on hazards and risks associated with the design of the structure, its construction and subsequent use and maintenance must be freely available to all members of the project team.

No one has a monopoly on the safest way to do things and previous experiences of other team members may add valuable contribution to the debate on health and safety.

Legislation

Construction (Design and Management) Regulations 1994

● *Regulation 13*

Code of Practice

Managing Health and Safety in Construction (HSG 224: ISBN 0 7176 2139 1)

As a Design Practice, are we legally responsible for the actions of our employees?

Yes. All employers have vicarious liability for their employees and the duties placed on designers apply to the employer of all employed Designers. If Designers are self-employed, then they are responsible individually for ensuring that they comply with the law.

Employers must ensure that their employees comply with the laws of CDM.

In order to clarify this situation, amendments to the CDM Regulations were made as a result of a Court of Appeal case which ruled that 'designers' were only those people who carried out designs. This implied that employers were *not* responsible for their employees and made the CDM Regulations, in respect of Designers' duties, almost unenforceable.

The Health and Safety Commission put forward an amendment to the Regulations which reinstated the original intent of the law, namely that 'Designer' meant Designers, their employers and those controlling design work when preparing designs.

Legislation

Construction (Design and Management) Regulations 1994

● *Regulation 2*

Construction (Design and Management) (Amendment) Regulations 2000

Code of Practice

Managing Health and Safety in Construction (HSG 224: ISBN 0 7176 2139 1)

As Designers, must we provide information on all hazards and risks associated with the project?

No. The CDM Regulations require Designers to take account of significant risks which a competent Contractor might *not* be aware of in respect of their designs.

All competent Contractors, for instance, should be aware of the hazards and risks of working at heights and the Designer does not need to give the Principal Contractor chapter and verse on the safety precautions for working at heights. However, the Designer should consider how to *reduce* the need to work at height and, if a particular sequence of construction is envisaged, then the Designer must provide this information to the Principal Contractor, via the Planning Supervisor.

Providing too much information on all hazards and risks of construction obscures the important detail about significant risks.

Contractors need to know about any specific materials or construction sequences planned in order to achieve the desired design effect of the building and with which they may not be overly familiar, e.g. the installation of glazed atria.

Legislation

Construction (Design and Management) Regulations 1994

● *Regulation 13*

Code of Practice

Managing Health and Safety in Construction (HSG 224: ISBN 0 7176 2139 1)

The Planning Supervisor insists that we co-operate with other Designers. How can we best achieve this?

Designers have to co-operate with the Planning Supervisor and other Designers and co-ordinate their work so that the principles of CDM for reducing hazards and risks in construction are met.

The reason that co-operation is needed between Designers is to ensure that hazards due to incompatibilities between different design functions are identified and addressed.

Co-operation and co-ordination can be achieved by:

- regular meetings of the Design Team and others
- agreement on the common principles of hazard and risk assessments, and the overriding requirement to reduce risks from design and construction
- regular reviews and on-going Design Team meetings to address changes in designs, developments in design, etc.
- co-ordinated design drawings that incorporate all design disciplines, e.g. Architects, Structural Engineers, Mechanical and Electrical Services and Interior Designers
- initial site survey meetings and co-ordinated site visits.

Designers need to ensure that their clients are informed of their responsibilities under the CDM Regulations and, in particular, that they must ensure that Designers have adequate resources to undertake their responsibilities. This means allowing enough time during the project design process for such co-ordination meetings to take place.

Legislation

Construction (Design and Management) Regulations 1994

- *Regulation 13*
- *Regulation 14*

Code of Practice

Managing Health and Safety in Construction (HSG 224: ISBN 0 7176 2139 1)

As a Designer, what do I not need to do under the CDM Regulations 1994?

Designers are not required to:

- take account of risks that were not reasonably foreseeable at the time the design was prepared
- provide information about unforeseeable risks
- provide information about insignificant risks
- specify construction methods unless the design proposed is unusual and a competent contractor may need information, e.g. a new construction technique or material used abroad and being introduced into this country
- monitor, manage, review or provide any health and safety management function over Contractors (other than that required under general health and safety laws or professional ethics)
- review and report on Contractors' health and safety performance
- keep copious notes and documents on all aspects of Design Risk Assessment other than conclusions about particular hazards and reasons for their design solutions.

Legislation

Construction (Design and Management) Regulations 1994

● *Regulation 13*

Code of Practice

Managing Health and Safety in Construction (HSG 224: ISBN 0 7176 2139 1)

Building Services Consultants (or Mechanical and Electrical Design and Build Contractors) advise that they do not have to produce Design Risk Assessments. Is this true?

No. Building Services Consultants, Mechanical and Electrical Design and Build Contractors, Public Health Engineers, etc., are all classed as Designers under the CDM Regulations and therefore the duties imposed under Regulation 13 apply to them.

Building services installations are often some of the most hazardous activities on site and it is essential that due consideration is given to the hazards and risks of such processes.

Services Designers must provide information to the Planning Supervisor regarding their proposed design solutions for the installation of plant and equipment, excavations for services, etc., and the Planning Supervisor must ensure that this information is co-ordinated throughout the Design Team.

The best method for Building Services Designers to provide this information is via Design Risk Assessments.

The true intent of the CDM Regulations can be seen with the co-ordination of building services information into the general design, as this will allow any conflicting processes to be considered and resolved prior to construction work commencing, e.g. rather than build solid walls and then have to chase out conduits for cabling, the design solution could incorporate hollow walls where the cabling could be run in the void thus preventing the need for chasing concrete and the subsequent health hazards of cement dust, noise and vibration, etc.

Building services Design Risk Assessments are required to be provided to the Principal Contractor so that they can address the identified hazards and risks in the Construction Phase Health and Safety Plan.

Specialist contractors are likely to be appointed to install building services and it is vital that the Principal Contractor has all available information so that he can ensure that hazards and risks that will affect the whole site and all operatives are considered, e.g. delivery of large and heavy plant and equipment to site, proposed lifting procedures, etc.

Legislation

Construction (Design and Management) Regulations 1994

● *Regulation 13*

Code of Practice

Managing Health and Safety in Construction (HSG 224: ISBN 0 7176 2139 1)

10

The Principal Contractor

What are the key duties of the Principal Contractor prior to the commencement of works on site?

The main duty of the Principal Contractor is to develop the Pre-tender Health and Safety Plan into a Construction Phase Health and Safety Plan. This must be done prior to the commencement of works on site.

The Principal Contractor, if appointed early enough, can add great value to the design process and should be consulted about construction sequences, methodology, available and suitable materials, etc.

If the Principal Contractor has any design responsibilities, he must provide Design Risk Assessments to the Planning Supervisor where appropriate, and he must ensure that he co-operates with all other Designers.

The Principal Contractor should have visited the site prior to the commencement of works and should liaise with the Planning Supervisor regarding any site-specific hazards and risks identified in the Pre-tender Health and Safety Plan.

Prior to the commencement of construction, the Principal Contractor should have identified and, if necessary, have appointed key Contractors who he believes to be competent and who possess the right resources to do the job. Regulations 8 and 9 state that:

> no person should arrange for a contractor to carry out or manage construction work unless he is reasonably satisfied that the contractor has the competence and resources to undertake the work and comply with legislation.

The requirement to assess competency and resources does not just rest with the Client — everyone who appoints Contractors has to satisfy themselves of their competency and resources.

If the Principal Contractor appoints the mechanical and electrical contractors then they must ensure their competency and this is best done prior to the commencement of construction works. Remember: 'every moment in planning saves three or four in execution'.

Legislation

Construction (Design and Management) Regulations 1994

- *Regulation 8*
- *Regulation 9*
- *Regulation 10*
- *Regulation 15*

Code of Practice

Managing Health and Safety in Construction (HSG 224: ISBN 0 7176 2139 1)

As Principal Contractor, what should we do if the Planning Supervisor has not prepared a Pre-tender Health and Safety Plan?

The purpose of the Pre-tender Health and Safety Plan is to provide information on health and safety hazards and risks which may be unusual and untypical in respect of the development project and to ensure that this information is received by the Contractor before he makes arrangements to carry out or manage the construction works.

By being in possession of such information you can plan the construction work safely and allow adequate resources, including operatives and financial, to do the job within the parameters set.

If the Planning Supervisor has failed to ensure that the Pre-tender Health and Safety Plan has been prepared, then they are in breach of their statutory duties.

You could inform the Client that you are unable to develop the Construction Phase Health and Safety Plan until you have the Pre-tender Health and Safety Plan. This will delay the start programme and will probably lead to the Client requiring action from the Planning Supervisor. You could diplomatically refer the Client to their duty to ensure competency and resources of the Planning Supervisor and indicate your concern regarding the former.

You could liaise directly with the nominated Planning Supervisor to obtain whatever information is available. It could be that the Planning Supervisor is having difficulty obtaining information from the Client and/or Design Team and is unable to proceed as they would wish. A joint consultation about the available information and the approach you intend to take could be all that is required to give you the details you need to develop the Construction Phase Health and Safety Plan into a form that satisfies Regulation 15 (4) and that allows the Client to comply with Regulation 10.

The Regulations do not specify how the information which forms the Health and Safety Plan should be put together, only what information it should contain.

The Pre-tender Health and Safety Plan does not have to be substantial in content, merely *specific* to the project in hand. Information could be annotated on project drawings or included in Employer Requirement documents.

Legislation

Construction (Design and Management) Regulations 1994

● *Regulation 15*

Code of Practice

Managing Health and Safety in Construction (HSG 224: ISBN 0 7176 2139 1)

Guidance

A Guide to Managing Health and Safety in Construction (HSE: ISBN 0 7176 07550)

If awarded the construction contract, is a Contractor automatically appointed Principal Contractor?

Not necessarily so. You must ensure that you are properly appointed as Principal Contractor by the Client, as this will clarify responsibilities.

The Pre-tender Health and Safety Plan may include a statement to the effect that the successful tenderer will be appointed Principal Contractor and must allow in his tender for such responsibilities.

A section may be included in the preliminaries to the Bill of Quantities or Specification for Works.

The Client cannot proceed with a construction project without appointing a Principal Contractor. Conflict and, more importantly, legal contraventions of the Regulations could occur if the Client thinks he has appointed a Principal Contractor but the successful tenderer has not assumed the responsibility.

Obtain appointments in writing and seek clear guidelines of what is expected of you.

Legislation

Construction (Design and Management) Regulations 1994

- *Regulation 6*

Code of Practice

Managing Health and Safety in Construction (HSG 224: ISBN 0 7176 2139 1)

Can a Contractor refuse to accept the position of Principal Contractor for a project?

Yes, but your Client might not be too impressed.

The appointment of Principal Contractor to a project is a legal duty which the Client has to fulfil. The Principal Contractor he chooses must operate a business/trade/profession as a Contractor and must be competent and have the resources to do the job. The Principal Contractor does *not* have to be the main or biggest Contractor on site but this is obviously preferable, as they will have more involvement with the site works.

If you refuse to accept the position of Principal Contractor you may be excluded from being awarded the contract. However, if you feel that you do not have the competency or resources to undertake the role, discuss this with the Client who may decide that someone else could be appointed.

If your refusal is due to inadequate financial recompense to fulfil the legal responsibilities discuss the matter with the Client because if the Client has not allowed for adequate resources to complete the job, he could be in breach of his legal duties under CDM.

Legislation

Construction (Design and Management) Regulations 1994

- *Regulation 6*
- *Regulation 8*
- *Regulation 9*

Code of Practice

Managing Health and Safety in Construction (HSG 224: ISBN 0 7176 2139 1)

Guidance

A Guide to Managing Health and Safety in Construction (HSE: ISBN 0 7176 07550)

Can there be more than one Principal Contractor on a project to which CDM applies?

There can be only one Principal Contractor at any one time on a project, although there may be many Main Contractors undertaking the works.

The Principal Contractor is a specific post required under the CDM Regulations with responsibility for managing and co-ordinating all of the construction phase health and safety issues. The Principal Contractor must be given overall responsibility for co-ordinating construction phases and, as this is such an important function, there can only be one such appointment.

Notwithstanding the above, at the same location there could be one or more different projects being carried out for different clients and, in these circumstances, one or more Principal Contractors could be appointed. Projects have to be distinct from each other and must not rely on one another for their viability and completion. If projects share common entrances or site access, need communal lifting equipment, share services to site, etc., then it is preferable to appoint one Principal Contractor with overall site management and co-ordinating responsibility so that these 'common resources' can be managed to the benefit of the site.

Each construction project could still have a Main Contractor responsible to their Client, but a representative should liaise with the Principal Contractor. Also, Planning Supervisors need to co-operate so that they can relay information to the respective Contractors regarding site and design hazards and risks generated by other parts of the project.

Legislation

Construction (Design and Management) Regulations 1994

- *Regulation 6*
- *Regulation 15*

Code of Practice

Managing Health and Safety in Construction (HSG 224: ISBN 0 7176 2139 1)

Asbestos has been identified within the building we are to refurbish. As Principal Contractor, what steps should we take?

Asbestos is a serious health hazard and is subject to strict health and safety controls.

Any asbestos present within the building should be identified within the Pre-tender Health and Safety Plan and an agreed procedure should be discussed with the Planning Supervisor and Client, prior to construction work commencing.

All asbestos identified as being at risk must be removed from the building prior to the main construction works and this is usually organised by the Client, Project Manager or Project Architect prior to the letting of the main contract.

If asbestos has been stripped out of the building, the Principal Contractor must obtain a copy of the Clean Air Certificate issued by the licensed Asbestos Removal Contractor. This should be obtained from the Planning Supervisor or Client. However, additional checks may be required to ensure that all asbestos has been removed.

If asbestos has been encapsulated within the building, it must be suitably labelled and identified on a drawing. Again, the Principal Contractor *must* be given detailed information on the location, type and condition of residual asbestos by the Planning Supervisor and must ensure that such information in respect of the hazards and risks of asbestos is contained in the Construction Phase Health and Safety Plan. In turn, this information must be given to all Contractors and operatives working on the site.

If asbestos is not to be removed prior to the commencement of construction works (not the preferred option), then the Principal Contractor must plan for the residual hazards and risks within the Construction Phase Health and Safety Plan and must prepare method statements for works to commence.

Preferably, the areas containing asbestos should be closed off, labelled as hazardous areas and designated 'Out of Bounds' until the removal takes place.

Removal of asbestos must be undertaken by licensed Contractors and unless secured, sealed-off work areas can be created for the removal of asbestos, the construction site should be cleared of all workers until declared safe and asbestos free, i.e. the Clean Air Certificate has been issued.

Finally, in whatever form asbestos is present on the construction site, the Principal Contractor should prepare and issue Risk Assessments identifying the hazards, risks and control measures.

Legislation

Construction (Design and Management) Regulations 1994

- *Regulation 11*
- *Regulation 14*
- *Regulation 15*
- *Regulation 16*

Control of Asbestos at Work Regulations 1987

Codes of Practice

Managing Health and Safety in Construction (HSG 224: ISBN 0 7176 2139 1)
Work with Asbestos Insulation, Asbestos Coating and Asbestos Insulating Board (HSE L28)
Control of Asbestos at Work (HSE L27)

11

The Pre-tender Health and Safety Plan

What is the Pre-tender Health and Safety Plan?

The Pre-tender Health and Safety Plan is a document which the Planning Supervisor has to ensure is prepared before any Contractor arranges to carry out or manage construction work.

The Regulations do not specifically require a Pre-tender Health and Safety Plan, merely that a Health and Safety Plan is available before construction works start. The term 'Pre-tender' has come into being to help differentiate that part of the Plan which the Planning Supervisor has to ensure is prepared and that part of the Plan which is developed by the Principal Contractor.

The Pre-tender Health and Safety Plan can also be known as the Pre-construction Health and Safety Plan.

The Pre-tender Health and Safety Plan should reflect *project specific* health and safety issues, specific Design Risk Assessments and any other specialist information which Contractors will need to know about in order to plan for health and safety during the construction phase. The Plan does not need to include every aspect of construction safety but must contain suitable and sufficient information on the project specific issues.

Legislation

Construction (Design and Management) Regulations 1994

- *Regulation 15*

Code of Practice

Managing Health and Safety in Construction (HSG 224: ISBN 0 7176 2139 1)

Guidance

A Guide to Managing Health and Safety in Construction (HSE: ISBN 0 7176 07550)
CDM Regulations — Practical Guidance for Planning Supervisors (CIRIA Report 173)

Does the Planning Supervisor actually have to prepare the Pre-tender Health and Safety Plan?

No. The Planning Supervisor need only ensure that it is prepared in time for Contractors to consider its implications before they start construction works.

The information for the Pre-tender Health and Safety Plan could be produced by each of the specialist Designers working on the project and the Planning Supervisor will need only to co-ordinate and collate the information and ensure that it is issued to the appropriate persons.

It would be sensible to discuss at the outset of the project who is expected to do what. If it is the Client's instruction that all Design Team members contribute to the Health and Safety Plan, this should be made clear early in the planning process.

Legislation

Construction (Design and Management) Regulations 1994

● *Regulation 15*

Code of Practice

Managing Health and Safety in Construction (HSG 224: ISBN 0 7176 2139 1)

How detailed does the Pre-tender Health and Safety Plan need to be?

The detail and size of the Pre-tender Health and Safety Plan will depend on the size and complexity of the project.

Its main purpose is to make clear the health and safety issues specific to the project so that tendering or negotiating Contractors can take account of the health and safety requirements and then explain their proposals for managing health and safety during the construction phase.

If sufficient information is included in the Pre-tender Health and Safety Plan, the intended Principal Contractor will have been able to give consideration to the relevant issues and to include adequate financial resources in his pricing strategy.

The Pre-tender Health and Safety Plan needs to be site specific, needs to include non-negotiable site safety standards and rules that the Client will impose, needs to cover environmental issues and any other unusual information peculiar to the proposed development.

Voluminous documents do not necessarily imply quality documents and the HSE is keen to see shorter, more site-specific documentation highlighting safety hazards which might not be obvious because of the nature of the site or the design.

Legislation

Construction (Design and Management) Regulations 1994

● *Regulation 15*

Code of Practice

Managing Health and Safety in Construction (HSG 224: ISBN 0 7176 2139 1)

Guidance

A Guide to Managing Health and Safety in Construction (HSE: ISBN 0 7176 07550)

What does the Pre-tender Health and Safety Plan need to include in order to comply with the Regulations?

The Pre-tender Health and Safety Plan should include the following:

- general description of the construction works comprised in the project
- details of the time within which it is intended that the project, and any intermediate stages, will be completed
- details of the project team, including Planning Supervisor, Designers and other Consultants
- details of existing plans, any Health and Safety File, etc.
- details of risks to health and safety of any person carrying out the construction work so far as such risks are known to the Planning Supervisor or are reasonably foreseeable or any such information as has been provided by the Designers, including Design Risk Assessments
- details of any Client requirements in relation to health and safety, e.g. safety goals for the project, Site Rules, permits to work, emergency procedures, management requirements, etc.
- such information as the Planning Supervisor knows or could ascertain by making reasonable enquiries regarding environmental considerations, on-site residual hazards, hazardous

buildings, overlap with the Client's business operation, site restrictions, etc.

- such information as the Planning Supervisor knows or could ascertain by making reasonable enquiries and which it would be reasonable for any Contractor to know in order to understand how he can comply with any requirements placed on him in respect of welfare by or under the relevant statutory provisions, e.g. availability of services, number of facilities required to be provided, and details of any shared occupancy of the site
- content and format of the expected Health and Safety File.

The Approved Code of Practice gives guidance as to what to include in the document and this can be summarised as:

- nature and description of project
- client considerations and management requirements
- existing environment and residual on-site risks
- existing drawings
- significant design principles and residual hazards and risks
- significant construction hazards.

The Planning Supervisor is expected to include (or to ensure is included) only that information which it is reasonable for them to *know* or which they could reasonably ascertain by making enquiries. The Regulations do not expect every aspect of potential hazard and risk to be known at the outset of the project but expects reasonable enquiries to be made.

The *competency* of the Planning Supervisor in foreseeing hazards and risks of the site, the existing building or the design and future use of the building would be investigated if obvious health and safety risks were not highlighted in the Pre-tender Health and Safety Plan.

Legislation

Construction (Design and Management) Regulations 1994

- *Regulation 15*

Code of Practice

Managing Health and Safety in Construction (HSG 224: ISBN 0 7176 2139 1)

Guidance

A Guide to Managing Health and Safety in Construction (HSE: ISBN 0 7176 07550)
CDM Regulations — Practical Guidance for Planning Supervisors (CIRIA Report 173)

What information should be available from the Client and what, and how, should it be included in the Pre-tender Health and Safety Plan?

The Client has a duty to provide information to the Planning Supervisor in order to enable the Planning Supervisor to fulfil their legal CDM duties.

The Planning Supervisor will need to discuss with the Client what information is currently available regarding the site or building to be developed, and what information *could* be ascertained by making reasonable enquiries.

Information will vary according to the complexity of the construction project, e.g. a greenfield site may have little available information while the refurbishment of an existing building will require detailed knowledge of the structure, surrounding area, building use, etc.

The Client should be able to provide the following information, arranging to have surveys carried out if necessary:

- contaminated land surveys
- existing services locations
- structural/building safety reports
- survey reports for hazardous substances, e.g. asbestos, lead and toxic substances

Case Study

A Planning Supervisor acts for one Client on many similar projects. A Pre-tender Health and Safety Plan format was agreed as a 'core' document for all projects, with one section dedicated to the site-specific information.

The contents of the Pre-tender Plan included:

- introduction and purpose of the plan
- project details and information
- health and safety objectives for the project
- responsibilities of all parties
- statutory requirements applicable to the project
- project specific health and safety information
- Site Rules
- requirements for managing health and safety
- information for the Health and Safety File.

- survey reports for hazardous areas, e.g. confined spaces
- survey reports for hazardous locations, e.g. fragile roof access
- local environmental conditions
- local hazardous areas, e.g. schools and major roadways
- current Health and Safety File
- intended occupancy details
- proposed Site Rules, e.g. existing Permit to Work systems
- proximity of water courses, transport systems, etc.
- history of any previous damage, e.g. fire damage, floods, etc.

The Client should be encouraged to commission surveys when the information produced would be vital to the planning of the project in respect of health and safety. The HSE will expect Clients to have taken responsibility for identifying hazardous conditions or substances, e.g. asbestos, and would consider prosecuting where there has been a blatant disregard to making information available.

Legislation

Construction (Design and Management) Regulations 1994

- *Regulation 11*
- *Regulation 15*

Code of Practice

Managing Health and Safety in Construction (HSG 224: ISBN 0 7176 2139 1)

Guidance

A Guide to Managing Health and Safety in Construction (HSE: ISBN 0 7176 07550)

Case Study

The Principal Contractor was undertaking refurbishment works during 1997 when he came across unexpected asbestos lagging to pipe work, previously hidden by a partition wall.

The project had to stop while notification for asbestos removal was made to the HSE. The HSE Inspector visited the site and wanted to know why the required 14 day notice had not been submitted. He formed the view that no planning for asbestos had been undertaken and that the Principal Contractor was trying to 'pull a fast one' to avoid the 14 day delay before works of removal could commence.

The HSE Inspector received the Pre-tender Health and Safety Plan and noted that an asbestos survey had been carried out but that the asbestos lagging on hidden pipes had not been noted and was unforeseen. The Principal Contractor had the current methods in place for the removal of any other asbestos found in the building and the Inspector was reasonably satisfied.

However, the investigation turned to the Planning Supervisor who was asked to account for the actions the Client took regarding commissioning asbestos surveys and how the Client judged the competency of the asbestos-surveying Contractor. The Inspector formed the view that it was reasonable for the Client to have commissioned a more detailed survey that should have included for the removal of wall and ceiling panels to ascertain whether asbestos was in any hidden areas, particularly in view of the building's age.

The Inspector issued an advisory letter to the Client stipulating that reasonable enquiries have to be made to obtain relevant information.

Who should receive a copy of the Pre-tender Health and Safety Plan?

The Regulations require the Pre-tender Health and Safety Plan to be provided to any Contractor before arrangements are made for that Contractor to carry out or manage construction work.

Therefore, the Pre-tender Health and Safety Plan should be issued to the following if involved in the project:

- all tendering Contractors for the main construction project
- all tendering Contractors for any specialist work packaged, e.g. Demolition Contractors
- specialist Mechanical and Electrical Contractors
- Design and Build Contractors
- Contractors operating partnership agreements.

There is no requirement under the CDM Regulations to provide a copy of the Pre-tender Health and Safety Plan to anyone else but it is good practice to provide a copy to the Client (unless they specifically request otherwise) and to the key members of the Design Team.

Legislation

Construction (Design and Management) Regulations 1994

- *Regulation 15*

Code of Practice

Managing Health and Safety in Construction (HSG 224: ISBN 0 7176 2139 1)

Guidance

A Guide to Managing Health and Safety in Construction (HSE: ISBN 0 7176 07550)

Does reference have to be made in the Pre-tender Health and Safety Plan to 'good practice' and legal requirements?

The Pre-tender Health and Safety Plan does not need to repeat legislation applicable to construction safety but it can include references to good practice where the Client and Planning Supervisor expect such standards to be adopted into the Construction Phase Health and Safety Plan.

It may be helpful to include references to legislation where unusual safety hazards exist or where legislation has recently been introduced with which the Contractors may not be fully conversant, e.g. Confined Spaces Regulations 1997.

The Planning Supervisor may have decided to include references to HSE Guidance Notes or Codes of Practice within the Pre-tender Plan or to other trade or professional guides. Of particular importance may be standards on Fire Safety, and reference to the Loss Prevention Council's code of practice on fire safety may stipulate the minimum standard of fire safety on the site for which the Contractor should cost.

Rather than include detailed references in the body of the Pre-tender Health and Safety Plan, it may be more practical and beneficial to include an Appendix to the Pre-tender Plan Health and Safety Plan which lists all relevant Legislation, Codes of Practice and Guidance available to the project.

Experience has shown that the Contractors are sometimes unaware of the extent of health and safety legislation and appreciate advice and information. The Planning Supervisor can create and develop a good working relationship with the Principal Contractor if they are perceived as helpful and supportive.

Legislation

Construction (Design and Management) Regulations 1994

● *Regulation 15*

Code of Practice

Managing Health and Safety in Construction (HSG 224: ISBN 0 7176 2139 1)

Guidance

A Guide to Managing Health and Safety in Construction (HSE: ISBN 0 7176 07550)

Does the Pre-tender Health and Safety Plan have to be issued to the Architect or Quantity Surveyor before it is issued to the Contractors?

No, unless terms of engagement stipulate that this shall be the case.

The Pre-tender Health and Safety Plan can be issued directly to the tendering Contractors by the Planning Supervisor as a separate document. As long as the Contractors have received the document in good time to allow them to consider the health and safety implications of the project, the residual risks, the control measures necessary and the financial consequences of providing any specific safety standards required by the Client and/or Planning Supervisor, it does not have to be sent out at the same time as other tendering packages.

Sending the Pre-tender Health and Safety Plan directly to the tendering Contractors could be good practice because it establishes a relationship between the Planning Supervisor and the prospective Contractors. Covering letters sent with the Plan could request addit- ional information to be submitted with the returned tender, e.g. Com- pany Safety Policy, Competency Questionnaire, Resource Plan, etc.

Legislation

Construction (Design and Management) Regulations 1994

● *Regulation 15*

Code of Practice

Managing Health and Safety in Construction (HSG 224: ISBN 0 7176 2139 1)

Guidance

A Guide to Managing Health and Safety in Construction (HSE: ISBN 0 7176 07550)

The Pre-tender Health and Safety Plan has been received by all tendering Contractors. What information should be received from them in respect of the Plan when they return their tenders?

The Pre-tender Health and Safety Plan provides information to Contractors on the project's health and safety requirements.

The tendering Contractors are expected to take account of the information when preparing their tender bids and must ensure that they have given adequate regard to the needs of the project.

If the Pre-tender Health and Safety Plan stipulates that a particular safety procedure must be followed, the Contractor must ensure that they highlight the matter in their documentation. They must *respond* to the Plan's requirements, e.g. if it stipulates a full-time Site Safety Officer then the Contractor must indicate that this has been understood and calculated for in the costings for the construction project.

The Planning Supervisor may have requested the tendering Contractors to stipulate specifically how they propose to undertake a particularly hazardous task, e.g. working adjacent to deep water, and the Contractor should ensure that they provide the relevant information.

An 'outline' Construction Phase Health and Safety Plan would be beneficial in determining the approach a Contractor is likely to take to health and safety on the project, but is not essential at this stage in the process.

Contractors have to demonstrate competency and resources to undertake construction works, and those who skimp on adequate information at such an early stage may have some difficulty demonstrating competence and resources.

The assessment of information supporting the returned tenders is a matter of judgement of those charged with the assessment task. Information should be related to the risks of the project and the Design Team need to demonstrate competence in differentiating between relevant and non-relevant but impressive information.

Be mindful of vast generic safety policy documents supporting tender bids. It will often be preferable to have slimmer documents that relate specifically to the project.

Legislation

Construction (Design and Management) Regulations 1994

● *Regulation 15*

Code of Practice

Managing Health and Safety in Construction (HSG 224: ISBN 0 7176 2139 1)

Guidance

A Guide to Managing Health and Safety in Construction (HSE: ISBN 0 7176 07550)

Can a project have more than one Pre-tender Health and Safety Plan?

Yes, if it is to be let in distinct phases.

If a project were to be let as two distinct packages — i.e. first a demolition contract and then a construction contract — and provided that there was a distinct break between the two phases, then a Pre-tender Health and Safety Plan will need to be produced for the demolition works and another one for the construction phase.

The Planning Supervisor may be competent to handle both aspects of the project and will prepare a specific Pre-tender Health and Safety Plan for the demolition works. This may be particularly prescriptive because demolition is a high-risk activity and the Client may require certain sequences and procedures to be followed. The Plan should be issued to all Contractors tendering for the demolition package.

The demolition works package will need its own Construction Phase Health and Safety Plan and, therefore, the Contractors must take account of the requirements of the Pre-tender Plan.

Once the demolition works have been completed and the design progressed for the new build project, the Planning Supervisor should prepare a second Pre-tender Health and Safety Plan which focuses on the construction phase. This Pre-tender Health and Safety Plan should then be issued to all the tendering Contractors for the new build project so that they can plan resources, safety procedures and standards for the project and cost them financially within the tendering process.

Legislation

Construction (Design and Management) Regulations 1994

- *Regulation 15*

Code of Practice

Managing Health and Safety in Construction (HSG 224: ISBN 0 7176 2139 1)

Guidance

A Guide to Managing Health and Safety in Construction (HSE: ISBN 0 7176 07550)

12

The Construction Phase Health and Safety Plan

What is the Construction Phase Health and Safety Plan?

The Construction Phase Health and Safety Plan is the document produced by the Principal Contractor which develops the Pre-tender Health and Safety Plan prepared by the Planning Supervisor.

The two documents make up the project's Health and Safety Plan as required by Regulation 15 of CDM.

The Health and Safety Plan is the foundation upon which the health and safety management of the construction phase needs to be based. A written plan clarifies who does what, who is responsible for what, what hazards and risks have been identified, how works shall be controlled, etc.

The Contractor appointed Principal Contractor must develop the Pre-tender Plan *before* construction works start so that it outlines the health and safety procedures which will be adopted during the construction phase.

The Construction Phase Plan must be site specific, i.e. it must cover issues that apply to the works to be carried out, include actual site personnel, site-specific emergency procedures, etc.

Regulation 15 (4) of CDM lists the information which must be included in the Construction Phase Plan as follows:

● arrangements for the project (including, where necessary, for management of construction work and monitoring compliance with the relevant statutory provisions) which will ensure, so far as is reasonably practicable, the health and safety of all persons at work carrying out the construction work and all persons who may be affected by the work of such persons at work, taking account of

○ the risks involved in the construction work

○ any activity of persons at work which is carried out, or will be carried out on or in premises where construction work is undertaken

○ any activity which may affect the health and safety of persons at work or other persons in the vicinity

● sufficient information about arrangements for the welfare of persons at work by virtue of the project to enable any Contractor to understand how he can comply with any requirements placed upon him in respect of welfare by or under the relevant statutory provision.

A Construction Phase Health and Safety Plan outline is shown in Appendix 13.

The Health and Safety Plan must remain in existence and must be relevant until the end of the construction works.

Legislation

Construction (Design and Management) Regulations 1994

● *Regulation 15*

Code of Practice

Managing Health and Safety in Construction (HSG 224: ISBN 0 7176 2139 1)

Guidance

A Guide to Managing Health and Safety in Construction (HSE: ISBN 0 7176 07550)

What format does the Construction Phase Health and Safety Plan have to have?

The Construction Phase Health and Safety Plan should be in a format which is:

- easy to use and to refer to
- understandable to those who need to use it
- easy to update
- easy to duplicate
- clear, concise and logical.

The Construction Phase Health and Safety Plan is needed *on site* and, therefore, should be robust and almost non-destructible. An A4 ring binder is a popular choice for keeping the information in order, as pages can be easily removed and photocopied for other Contractors as necessary and, more importantly, it can be easily updated.

The Construction Phase Health and Safety Plan would not be particularly useful on computer disk on the site because access to its information may be restricted.

The Construction Phase Health and Safety Plan need not be all written words — often the use of diagrams, pictograms and cartoons are very effective at explaining health and safety messages.

The Plan should not contain every health and safety procedure known to man but only those *applicable* to the site. This should prevent it from becoming unwieldy and will not discourage people from reading it. It is perfectly acceptable to cross-reference to other documents within the Plan, e.g. the detailed Risk Assessment manual, or to the COSHH (Control of Substances Hazardous to Health Regulations 1999) manual. If site safety procedures are reliant on safety procedures specified in other documents, then copies of these must be available on site.

Legislation

Construction (Design and Management) Regulations 1994

- *Regulation 15*

Code of Practice

Managing Health and Safety in Construction (HSG 224: ISBN 0 7176 2139 1)

Guidance

A Guide to Managing Health and Safety in Construction (HSE: ISBN 0 7176 07550)

Does a copy of the Health and Safety Plan have to be given to every person working on the site, the Client, the Planning Supervisor, etc.?

No. The Client must be given a copy of the Plan so that they can be satisfied that it has been prepared and that it complies with the Regulations.

There is no duty to give a copy to the Planning Supervisor unless the Planning Supervisor is acting instead of the Client in assessing its adequacy before construction works can start. In this case, there would be no need to send one to the Client.

The CDM Regulations require the Principal Contractor to provide information to all persons working on or resorting to the site in respect of health and safety issues.

As the Health and Safety Plan contains valuable information on site health and safety matters it makes sense to issue the document to as many people as practicable. However, that may become expensive and some operatives may be on site for only a few days.

Site safety rules should be issued to all individual operatives and could be issued to all employers/Contractors/employees during site induction training.

Specific Risk Assessments should be issued to the Ganger or Foreman, with instructions that he is responsible for ensuring that all his gang/team are made aware of hazards and risks and of the protective measures needed to control the risks.

Copies of relevant information could be displayed in the messroom, site office and site canteen, e.g. location of first aid kit, names of companies with trained first aiders.

Key aspects of the Health and Safety Plan can be issued to safety representatives, site foremen, etc., with guidance on how and where they can access the full Health and Safety Plan and supporting information, documentation, e.g. Company Safety Policy, HSE Codes of Practice, etc.

A practical way of disseminating site health and safety information is to convene a weekly site safety forum or committee, requiring a Foreman or representative from every Contractor or self-employed person on site to attend, using the meeting to review site health and safety issues and to discuss forthcoming works on the programme, new site safety rules, etc.

Legislation

Construction (Design and Management) Regulations 1994

- *Regulation 16*
- *Regulation 17*
- *Regulation 18*

Code of Practice

Managing Health and Safety in Construction (HSG 224: ISBN 0 7176 2139 1)

Guidance

A Guide to Managing Health and Safety in Construction (HSE: ISBN 0 7176 07550)

Case Study

A major shop-fitting Contractor acted as a Principal Contractor and developed a comprehensive Health and Safety Plan. A summary version was produced which covered Site Rules, Emergency Procedures, Fire Safety, Personal Protective Equipment, Signing in Procedures, etc., and this document was given to all operatives and visitors to site who underwent the site safety induction training. Additional notices were displayed in the canteen, mess room, site office and at the entrance to the site.

Each major Contractor on site was given a full copy of the Health and Safety Plan and was required to sign a record to that effect. They were then required to ensure that all relevant information regarding health and safety had been provided to their site operatives.

The Principal Contractor introduced an auditing system which regularly checked how, to whom and when the Contractor issued the information.

As Principal Contractor, I intend to revise the original Construction Phase Health and Safety Plan. Do I need to tell the Planning Supervisor or the Client?

Only if your revisions are due to design changes. The Planning Supervisor has to ensure that Designers conduct Risk Assessments and need to be sure that these have been done. They rely on the Principal Contractor to inform them. It should be beneficial to have a discussion with the Planning Supervisor regarding the proposed changes.

There is no duty to advise the Client of any changes to the Construction Phase Health and Safety Plan under the CDM Regulations and there is no duty on the Client to check that you have made changes or updates to the Plan.

However, you will want to create a good impression and to demonstrate competence, so it would be advisable to keep the Client informed. This could be done by way of project meetings and it would be wise to minute a health and safety section on the agenda.

The Client and the Design Team or other professional advisers will need to be briefed on any changes to the Construction Phase Health and Safety Plan which could affect their safety, e.g. changes to Site Rules, restricted areas of the site, etc.

Legislation

Construction (Design and Management) Regulations 1994

- *Regulation 15*
- *Regulation 16*
- *Regulation 17*
- *Regulation 18*

Code of Practice

Managing Health and Safety in Construction (HSG 224: ISBN 0 7176 2139 1)

Guidance

A Guide to Managing Health and Safety in Construction (HSE: ISBN 0 7176 07550)

What is the best way to update the Construction Phase Health and Safety Plan without it becoming complicated or confusing?

The Construction Phase Health and Safety Plan is the document which sets out the health and safety management of the construction phase of the project. It must be a document which outlines what special health and safety precautions are to be taken to ensure the safety of everyone on the construction project and must be updated to reflect any changes to the working procedures, management systems, welfare facilities, etc., which happen on the site.

If the majority of the Construction Phase Health and Safety Plan has been agreed before the commencement of the construction works there will be little need to change substantial parts of it. Details of site management, emergency procedures and welfare facilities may not change during the construction phase if they have been well thought through at the beginning.

If the Construction Phase Health and Safety Plan needs to be updated it should be done by adding information clearly and removing old information so as to avoid confusion. For instance, the names of the trained first aiders may change. The new ones should be added to the Plan and the old ones removed. If the location of the first aid kit has changed, this should be included.

The most important thing about the Construction Phase Health and Safety Plan is that the information contained in it is made available to all operatives on site — the simpler the updates the easier things will be to understand.

Risk Assessments and Method Statements should be included at the back of the Plan, making it easy to add new information.

If the Principal Contractor decides to implement a new Permit to Work procedure for a specific activity which has only recently come to light, then this Permit to Work system must be clearly explained in the Construction Phase Health and Safety Plan.

An aspect of the Construction Health and Safety Plan which will need to be constantly kept under review, and updated when necessary, will be the Fire Safety Plan. As construction work progresses, exit routes may become altered, e.g. by permanent partitioning, etc. Alterations must be depicted clearly on the Fire Safety Plan.

The Principal Contractor should ensure that, perhaps once a week, time is set aside to review the Construction Phase Health and Safety Plan and any relevant changes which are made must be *communicated* to site operatives by way of the arrangements made for ensuring health and safety issues are considered, e.g. at the weekly site Contractors' meeting.

Feedback from site operatives on health and safety matters should be considered and the Construction Health and Safety Plan should be amended or updated to take into account operatives' concerns, ideas and suggestions as to how the site could be improved from a health and safety point of view.

Generic Risk Assessments will need to be reviewed and updated to incorporate site-specific issues. These should then be kept in the Appendix of the Construction Phase Health and Safety Plan, together with any associated Method Statements. Individual Risk Assessments can be issued to specific operatives as necessary, or more importantly, to the Contractor Foreman so that he can assess what safety precautions need to be followed by his team.

Legislation

Construction (Design and Management) Regulations 1994

● *Regulation 15*

Code of Practice

Managing Health and Safety in Construction (HSG 224: ISBN 0 7176 2139 1)

Guidance

A Guide to Managing Health and Safety in Construction (HSE: ISBN 0 7176 07550)

Is the Fire Safety Plan a separate document?

No, the Fire Safety Plan can be an integral part of the Construction Phase Health and Safety Plan.

The Fire Safety Plan should identify fire risks throughout the site, e.g.:

- combustible materials
- use of hot flame equipment
- use of liquid petroleum gas (LPG)
- use of combustible substances
- storage and use of any explosive materials and substances
- sources of ignition, e.g. smoking
- use of heaters.

Once the potential fire risks are identified — i.e. where, when, why and how a fire *could* start on site (or the surrounding area, yards, outbuildings) — the Fire Safety Plan should include precautions and procedures to be adopted to *reduce* the risks of fire. These could include:

- operating a Hot Works Permit system
- banning smoking on site in all areas other than the approved messroom
- controlling and authorising the use of combustible materials and substances
- providing non-combustible storage boxes for chemicals
- minimising the use of liquid petroleum gas and designating external storage areas
- controlling the siting and use of heaters and drying equipment
- operating a Permit to Work system for gas and electrical works.

Having identified the potential risks and the ways to minimise them, there will always be some residual risk of fire. The Fire Safety Plan should then contain the Emergency Procedures for dealing with an outbreak of fire, namely:

- types and location of Fire Notices
- the location, number and type of fire extinguishers provided throughout the site
- the means of raising the alarm
- identification of fire exit routes from the site and surrounding areas
- access routes for emergency services
- procedure for raising the alarm
- assembly point/muster point.

The Fire Safety Plan should also contain the procedures to be taken on site to protect against arson, e.g.:

- erection of high fencing/hoarding to prevent unauthorised entry
- fenced or caged storage areas for all materials, particularly those combustible
- site lighting
- use of CCTV
- continuous fire checks of the site, particularly at night if site security is used.

Procedures for the storage and disposal of waste need to be included, as waste is one of the highest sources of fire on construction sites.

Materials used for the construction of temporary buildings should be fire protected or non-combustible whenever possible, e.g. 30 minute fire protection. The siting of temporary buildings must be considered early in the site planning stage as it is best to site them at least ten metres away from the building being constructed or renovated.

Having completed the Fire Safety Plan, a sketch plan of the building indicating fire points, assembly point, fire exit routes, emergency services' access route to site, etc., should be completed and attached to the Plan. The sketch plan (which could be an Architect's outline existing drawing) should be displayed at all fire points and main fire exit routes and must be included in any Site Rules/information handed out at induction training.

Legislation

Construction (Design and Management) Regulations 1994

● *Regulation 15*

Code of Practice

Managing Health and Safety in Construction (HSG 224: ISBN 0 7176 2139 1)

Guidance

Fire Prevention on Construction Sites — Joint Code of Practice: Loss Prevention Council
Fire Safety in Construction Works (HSE HS(G) 168)
Health & Safety in Construction (HSE HS(G) 150)

What criticisms does the Health and Safety Executive have of Construction Phase Health and Safety Plans?

The HSE have raised many concerns about the quality of Construction Phase Health and Safety Plans, in particular regarding the general content which is often not relevant to the project in hand. They would prefer thinner but more site-specific documents.

Some of the common deficiencies are itemised as follows:

● Activities are not assessed, i.e. those activities with health and safety risks which affect the whole site or specific trades: e.g. storage and distribution of materials, movement of vehicles, pedestrian access ways, removal of waste, provision and use of common mechanical plant, provision and use of temporary services, commissioning and testing procedures, etc.

- Management arrangements do not focus sufficiently on the role of Risk Assessments.
- Site supervisors and managers do not have reasonable knowledge of safety, health and welfare requirements and standards.
- Site supervisors and managers are not familiar with the contents of the Construction Phase Health and Safety Plan.
- Monitoring arrangements are overlooked or the 'competent' person performing this role is not suitably qualified.
- Details of welfare provision is limited to a couple of lines of the Plan. It should cover, in explicit detail, the requirements and implementation of Schedule 6 Construction (Health, Safety & Welfare) Regulations 1996.
- Fire precautions, including arrangements for the fire alarm system (if required) and emergency lighting, are often over-looked.
- The implication for health and safety of tight time-scales for the project are not fully addressed in the Plan. The Plan often fails to recognise that shortening a construction programme increases both the amount of material stored on site and the number of operatives on site, all of which leads to restricted work space, inadequate supervision, poor co-ordination and control, etc.

The HSE Inspectors believe that all of the above must be considered before works commence on site, and that if a Construction Phase Health and Safety Plan does not adequately address them, a Client should not approve the document under Regulation 10 of the CDM Regulations.

Legislation

Construction (Design and Management) Regulations 1994

- *Regulation 15*

Code of Practice

Managing Health and Safety in Construction (HSG 224: ISBN 0 7176 2139 1)

Guidance

A Guide to Managing Health and Safety in Construction (HSE: ISBN 0 7176 07550)

What other health and safety legislation must the Construction Phase Health and Safety Plan address?

The Construction Phase Health and Safety Plan is a specific requirement of the CDM Regulations but the CDM Regulations are not the only health and safety legislation applicable to construction projects.

The Construction Phase Health and Safety Plan must make reference to the monitoring of compliance with the relevant statutory provisions which are applicable to the construction site, namely, but not exhaustively, the following:

- Health & Safety at Work Etc. Act 1974
- Health & Safety (First Aid) Regulations 1981
- Control of Asbestos at Work Regulations 1987
- Noise at Work Regulations 1989
- Electricity at Work Regulations 1989
- Construction (Head Protection) Regulations 1989
- Manual Handling Operations Regulations 1992
- Personal Protective Equipment Regulations 1992
- Gas Safety (Installation and Use) Regulations 1994
- Reporting of Injuries, Diseases and Dangerous Occurrences Regulations 1995
- Health & Safety (Consultation with Employees) Regulations 1996

Case Study

A recent routine site investigation by an HSE Construction Inspector highlighted that an unacceptable Construction Phase Health and Safety Plan had been prepared for the project. The Plan was not site specific and included a large amount of irrelevant information. The HSE Inspector wanted to know who had approved the Plan. The Client thought the Planning Supervisor had but possessed no written record of this and so, ultimately, the Client is being held responsible for allowing works to start without a Construction Phase Health and Safety Plan complying with Regulation 15 (4).

- Construction (Health, Safety & Welfare) Regulations 1996
- Health & Safety (Safety Signs and Signals) Regulations 1996
- Control of Lead at Work Regulations 1998
- Confined Spaces Regulations 1997
- Provision and Use of Work Equipment Regulations 1998
- Lifting Operations & Lifting Equipment Regulations 1998
- Management of Health & Safety at Work Regulations 1999
- Control of Substances Hazardous to Health Regulations 1999.

Not all of the above legislation will apply to a construction site — it depends on the complexity of the project and the type of work to be carried out. The Principal Contractor must be aware of which Regulations are applicable to the works and must ensure that both their own employees and other Contractors are complying with the requirements where necessary.

If the Principal Contractor is not familiar with the requirements of the legislation, he should seek expert guidance from in-house safety officers or external Consultants. The Planning Supervisor should be able to give good practical guidance if asked to do so.

The duty to comply with some of the Regulations may fall to the Principal Contractor where the activity will affect all operatives and visitors to the site, e.g. conducting a COSHH Assessment on dust.

Legislation

Construction (Design and Management) Regulations 1994

- *Regulation 15*

Code of Practice

Managing Health and Safety in Construction (HSG 224: ISBN 0 7176 2139 1)

Case Study

The Principal Contractor identified that several trades would be using power tools at the same time and, although individual Contractors had provided ear defenders to their own employees, there were other operatives in the vicinity who would be subjected to high noise levels over a prolonged period. The Principal Contractor carried out a noise assessment of all the tools in operation at any one time and concluded that the noise level in the site was over the legal limit (90 dB (A)) and that, therefore, he must take action to reduce the noise levels. He reorganised the work programme so that only half the number of tools were in use at any one time, thereby reducing the overall noise level to below the legal limit. This action was preferable to issuing all workers on the site with ear defenders, i.e. he had controlled the noise at source — step one of the Hierarchy of Risk Control.

Does the Construction Phase Health and Safety Plan have to make reference to any other legislation other than health and safety?

Legally, no. The Plan is prepared to address health and safety issues and it would not contravene the law if this is all it did.

However, the law sets down only the *minimum* standards that must be adopted in any situation and it is good practice, and often beneficial from a business point of view, to set down higher standards than those legally required. The Construction Phase Health and Safety Plan could therefore address key environmental protection issues and make reference to the relevant legislation, namely:

- Clean Air Acts 1956 and 1968
- Control of Pollution Act 1974
- Environmental Protection Act 1990
- Environmental Protection (Duty of Care) Regulations 1991
- Environment Act 1995
- Special Waste Regulations 1996.

The above list is not exhaustive but indicates the key legislation that could be considered in the Construction Phase Health and Safety Plan.

For instance, a policy dealing with environmental noise could be adopted that sets out to reduce the noise nuisance that can be caused to residents in the vicinity from the use of machines, e.g. generators, diggers, pneumatic drills, the use of tools and equipment such as power tools, chasing works, power hammers, etc.

It is essential for the Principal Contractor to know exactly how waste from the site will be taken and to where. Waste must go to licensed landfill sites and 'Duty of Care' Notices must accompany the waste. Any special waste, e.g. asbestos or clinical waste, must be dealt with separately and be taken to authorised sites or incinerators. A Principal Contractor who knowingly allows waste to be fly-tipped will be guilty of an offence.

The storage of 'special' waste on site must be carefully managed so as to avoid health hazards to operatives and pollution to the environment, which could lead to contaminated land.

'Special' waste includes construction and demolition waste, paints, adhesives, sealants and varnishes. It also includes any substances and materials which display any of the following properties:

- explosive
- flammable
- harmful
- carcinogenic
- infections
- oxidising
- irritant
- toxic
- corrosive
- eco-toxic.

The Construction Phase Health and Safety Plan should include procedures for how and where the waste will be stored, who is authorised to move it, who will sign the 'consignment notes', who will approve waste removal Contractors, etc.

Site waste is an excellent example of the inter-relationship between health and safety and environmental issues.

Legislation

As listed above plus:

Alkali etc. Works Regulation Act 1906
Rivers (Prevention of Pollution) Act 1951
Public Health Acts 1936 and 1961
Local Government Act 1972
Highways Act 1980
Control of Pollution (Amendment) Act 1989
Planning (Hazardous Substances) Act 1990

Town & Country Planning Act 1990
Water Resources Act 1991
Noise & Statutory Nuisance Act 1993

European Directives

Environmental Impact Assessment Directive 1985 and 1997
Hazardous Waste Directive 1991
Waste Directive 1975
Waste Directive 1991

Does the Construction Phase Health and Safety Plan have to be included in the Client's Health and Safety File?

No. The Construction Phase Health and Safety Plan details what safety precautions are to be adopted during the course of construction. Once the construction work has finished the Plan is, to all intents and purposes, redundant, and provides little useful information to the future use and occupancy of the building.

The Construction Phase Health and Safety Plan should contain a section on how information will be collected for the Health and Safety File and who will be responsible for relaying it to the Planning Supervisor.

If the Health and Safety Plan identifies that an area within the site will be a confined space and includes a system of work (Method Statement) of how to enter and work in the confined space safely, this information could be passed onto the Planning Supervisor for inclusion in the Health and Safety File, as it would have relevance to the safe use of the building/land in the future.

Discuss with the Planning Supervisor early on in the project what information you are expected to provide, in what format, etc.

Legislation

Construction (Design and Management) Regulations 1994

- *Regulation 15*
- *Regulation 16*

Code of Practice

Managing Health and Safety in Construction (HSG 224: ISBN 0 7176 2139 1)

Part 4

On site

Chapter summary

Chapter 13 The Client

Covers the main responsibilities at this stage of the project, and the appointment of 'Client Directs' are covered in the question and answer format.

Chapter 14 The Designer

Does the Designer have health and safety responsibilities when a project is on site? How does CDM apply to Structural Engineers? On-going design issues are a few of the subjects covered.

Chapter 15 The Planning Supervisor

Is there a need to visit site during construction? What information needs to be gathered dealing with ongoing design issues?

Chapter 16 The Principal Contractor

What needs to be covered in the Method Statements and Risk Assessments? Does the Planning Supervisor need to have copies? Welfare facilities, general health and safety management, training and information, and failure to discharge duties are also covered in this chapter.

Chapter 17 Contractors

Duties extend to Contractors on site and this chapter looks at issues, duties and responsibilities under CDM of all Contractors appointed to projects, either as Sub-contractors to the Principal Contractor or as appointed by the Client.

Chapter 18 Practical on-site initiatives

Examples of some of the health and safety initiatives that have been adopted on site to improve safety. Reference to the HSE's Working Well Together Campaign and relevant website address are issues covered in this chapter.

13

The Client

What are a Client's main responsibilities once the project has started the construction phase?

Once a Client has confirmed that a Construction Phase Health and Safety Plan complying with Regulation 15 (4) has been produced then construction works can start.

The Client has few responsibilities under CDM once the construction phase has started, as all site safety management issues fall to the Principal Contractor.

The Client's main responsibility will be to ensure that any subsequent design changes have been notified to the Planning Supervisor so that they can continue to update the Principal Contractor regarding Design Risk Assessments, etc.

The Client should ensure that the Principal Contractor has adequate resources to complete the project, especially if design changes have taken place post-construction start. Extending the construction phase may be appropriate so that the Principal Contractor has sufficient time to coordinate others in respect of new materials, construction sequences, etc.

The Client could also assist the Planning Supervisor in obtaining suitable information for the Health and Safety File and could make any new information on the site conditions, existing services, other construction projects, etc. available to the Planning Supervisor.

Legislation

Construction (Design and Management) Regulations 1994

- *Regulation 11*
- *Regulation 12*

Code of Practice

Managing Health and Safety in Construction (HSG 224: ISBN 0 7176 2139 1)

Is the Client responsible for supervising the Principal Contractor?

No. The CDM Regulations place no responsibility on the Client for supervising and monitoring the Principal Contractor once works have started.

The Client should have exercised his responsibilities under CDM prior to the commencement of construction works in so far as the Client has to appoint a competent Principal Contractor.

There is not duty under CDM to monitor the Principal Contractor's compliance with the Construction Phase Health and Safety Plan and, provided it complied with Regulation 15 (4) prior to the commencement of works, there are no further duties on any member of the Design Team, or Client, to monitor health and safety during the construction phase.

However, contract documentation agreed between the Client and the Principal Contractor may stipulate that the Client, or his representative, will independently monitor health and safety standards on site. This will be a contractual or employers' requirement and will be outside of the scope of the CDM Regulations.

Legislation

Construction (Design and Management) Regulations 1994

- *Regulation 10*
- *Regulation 15*

Code of Practice

Managing Health and Safety in Construction (HSG 224: ISBN 0 7176 2139 1)

What are the Client's responsibilities for 'Client Direct' appointments to the Construction Phase?

It is quite common for Clients to appoint specialist Contractors to a construction project by direct negotiation or specialised tendering process. These may be Mechanical and Electrical Contractors, specialist finishing Contractors or other specialist Contractors.

The requirement of CDM is that no person shall arrange for a Contractor to carry out or manage construction works, unless they are satisfied that they have the competence and resources to undertake the works.

Therefore, if the Client appoints a Contractor directly then the Client is responsible for ensuring that the Contractor meets any competency and resourcing requirements. The Principal Contractor would not be responsible, as they would not have made the appointment.

The Client must ensure that the 'Client Direct' appointee is fully aware of the fact that they will be working on the construction site under the management and supervision of the Principal Contractor.

The Planning Supervisor will be responsible for ensuring that the 'Client Direct' Contractor is provided with a copy of the Pre-tender Health and Safety Plan and the Principal Contractor shall ensure that they receive the Construction Phase Health and Safety Plan.

The 'Client Direct' Contractor will *not* be Principal Contractor and will not need to produce a Construction Phase Health and Safety Plan, although they will need to produce a safety plan, Method Statements and Risk Assessments for the works they are to carry out.

The Client should ask the Planning Supervisor to assist with the coordination of this information.

If the 'Client Direct' Contractor acts as a Designer, e.g. Mechanical Design and Build Contractor, then the responsibilities of Designer under CDM apply and they will need to assess hazards and risks from their design.

Again, the Client must only appoint competent Designers and must ensure that they assess this before making the appointment.

Legislation

Construction (Design and Management) Regulations 1994

- *Regulation 6*
- *Regulation 8*
- *Regulation 9*
- *Regulation 13*
- *Regulation 15*
- *Regulation 19*

Code of Practice

Managing Health and Safety in Construction (HSG 224: ISBN 0 7176 2139 1)

Asbestos has been found within the site after works of construction commenced. As Client, do I have any responsibilities?

The Principal Contractor is responsible for ensuring that all aspects of health and safety are managed on the site, including any unforeseen events, hazards and risks to Contractors and others.

If the construction project involves refurbishing an existing building and the Client, as employer, still has employees working in the building, then they will have responsibilities under the Control of Asbestos at Work Regulations 1987 (as amended) and must act to ensure the safety of their employees and others.

Under Regulation 11 CDM, the Client has a duty to provide information to the Planning Supervisor about the state or condition of any premises and a review should be undertaken to establish why such information was not available prior to the commencement of construction works. If it can be shown that the Client purposely ignored this duty then they would be in breach of the law.

On a practical basis, if the Client is made aware of the presence of asbestos materials, he must liaise with all appropriate personnel and agree a revised construction timetable so that operatives are not put at risk during the asbestos removal. There will be a minimum 14 day notification to the HSE for asbestos removal and if the asbestos on site cannot be contained, or if it may have contaminated surfaces, etc., then the site will need to be closed down for safety reasons. The Client must acknowledge the severity of the health risk and must not place undue pressure on the Principal Contractor to continue works.

The HSE is keen to convey the fact that Clients are the driving force behind improved health and safety standards in construction.

Legislation

Construction (Design and Management) Regulations 1994

- *Regulation 11*
- *Regulation 15*
- *Regulation 16*

Control of Asbestos at Work Regulations 1987 (amended)

Code of Practice

Managing Health and Safety in Construction (HSG 224: ISBN 0 7176 2139 1)

Case Study

HSE Inspectors successfully prosecuted two companies under the CDM Regulations for failing to manage asbestos on site. Fines were more than £20,000.

The Client had failed to conduct a proper survey of a boiler house which contained asbestos and in which work was to be carried out. Had a suitable survey been carried out it would have revealed the presence of asbestos. The Client was prosecuted and fined £10,000 plus nearly £5,000 in costs.

The Contractor was also prosecuted for putting its workers at risk by exposing them to asbestos.

Neither company had followed proper procedures. The Client had relied on third-hand information from another Contractor, which included analysis results from unrepresentative samples. Pipework was dismantled by operatives and put in black sacks. No one had any personal protective equipment.

Asbestos was discovered when a licensed Asbestos Contractor was called to site and air samples revealed large amounts of asbestos fibres in the air.

The HSE commented that the Client had a legal duty to carry out a proper survey, relay information to the Contractor and employ competent persons to remove the risk.

It has become apparent that further investigative works are required on the site to establish whether the land is contaminated. As Client, am I responsible for arranging this?

The question to really ask here is why the likelihood of a contaminated site was *not* discovered prior to the commencement of the construction phase. The Client is responsible under CDM for providing the Planning Supervisor with information regarding the state or condition of any premises at or on which construction work is to be carried out. The Planning Supervisor has a duty to relay this information to the Principal Contractor in the Pre-tender Health and Safety Plan.

Should evidence be discovered that potentially contaminated land exists, the Principal Contractor shall take steps to ensure the health and safety of all operatives and persons resorting to the site.

The Client will be responsible for commissioning a suitable survey so that information on hazards and risks can be provided to the Principal Contractor. The Client may prefer to commission the Architect, Project Manager or Principal Contractor to organise the investigation works, but whether they do so or not, the Client is responsible for ensuring that they do not abdicate their responsibilities for health and safety within the project process and the Client must ensure that the Principal Contractor has adequate resources and the competency to deal with the hazards discovered.

Should the information come to the attention of the HSE Inspector, they will be particularly interested to establish what actions the Client took prior to the commencement of works. They would also be interested in the role of the Design Team and the Planning Supervisor.

Legislation

Construction (Design and Management) Regulations 1994

- *Regulation 11*
- *Regulation 15*
- *Regulation 16*

Code of Practice

Managing Health and Safety in Construction (HSG 224: ISBN 0 7176 2139 1)

14

The Designer

As a Designer, do I have any responsibility for site safety matters during construction?

No. There is no legal responsibility on Designers to undertake any safety auditing role.

Obviously, frequent visits to the site will give ample opportunity to identify any breaches of health and safety rules and where these are noted they should be reported to the Site Agent for their action.

Professional conduct codes require members to act responsibly when safety breaches are encountered and to report them. You do not have to tell the Site Agent what to do to put them right unless you have specific information available about a material or product.

Health and safety legislation imposes a duty on all persons to take responsibility for reporting or taking action in respect of health and safety hazards or contraventions.

Legislation

Construction (Design and Management) Regulations 1994

● *Regulation 13*

Code of Practice

Managing Health and Safety in Construction (HSG 224: ISBN 0 7176 2139 1)

As the Designer, what are my key responsibilities under the CDM Regulations during the construction phase of the Project?

The predominant duty of a Designer under CDM is to ensure that due regard is given to the health and safety impact of their designs.

Designers need to follow the Hierarchy of Risk Control, namely:

- eliminate the hazard and risk at source
- substitute for a lesser risk
- protect the whole workforce
- protect the individual.

Often, the design process carries on during the construction phase with Designers making alterations to designs and site conditions may vary to what was expected. In these instances, the Designer must ensure that revisions to drawings or schemes consider health and safety implications, where appropriate, and new Design Risk Assessments will be required. These should be passed to the Planning Supervisor so that they can be integrated into the Construction Plans.

The Designer must provide the Planning Supervisor with information on the design, specifications, etc., for the Health and Safety File. Therefore, revisions to schemes should be recorded so that accurate information is available for future reference.

Designers should take responsibility for ensuring that design information, etc., is made available to the Planning Supervisor during the course of the project — do not wait until completion. Materials' datasheets, revised drawings, operating and maintenance manuals can all be passed on when available. This will enable the Planning Supervisor to review the information and request further details if necessary, so as to ensure that a comprehensive and meaningful Health and Safety File can be produced for the project.

Legislation

Construction (Design and Management) Regulations 1994

- *Regulation 13*

Code of Practice

Managing Health and Safety in Construction (HSG 224: ISBN 0 7176 2139 1)

As a Structural Engineer, what are my key duties under CDM during the construction phase?

As a Structural Engineer you are classed as a Designer under the CDM Regulations and your duties are as outlined in Regulation 13.

During construction works there will inevitably be regular site visits and inspections of the works undertaken by the specialist Contractors on site. Design or specification alterations will need to be assessed with health and safety implications in mind, and amendments made to structural drawings and specifications, etc.

Major health and safety considerations should have been addressed during the planning stage and the information contained in the Pre-tender Health and Safety Plan. The Principal Contractor would then have developed these hazards and risks within the Construction Phase Health and Safety Plan.

The Structural Engineer should provide Design Risk Assessments and must consider sequences of demolition, construction, erection, etc.

If further structural design works are sub-contracted to a specialist Contractor, e.g. Steel Fabricator, then they are also classed as Designers under CDM and further Design Risk Assessments are required.

Temporary works are also designs under the Regulations and if the Structural Engineer is requested to design structures to enhance stability of a building, etc., then the Designer duties under Regulation 13 apply.

Information must be collated for the Health and Safety File and be passed to the Planning Supervisor. Of particular importance will be information on 'reverse construction', i.e. demolition, as Designers have to give due consideration to the future use, cleaning and demolition of structures. Examples of relevant information will include past tensioned members, unusual stability concepts, load-bearing structures, and alterations which have changed the structure.

Legislation

Construction (Design and Management) Regulations 1994

● *Regulation 13*

Code of Practice

Managing Health and Safety in Construction (HSG 224: ISBN 0 7176 2139 1)

As a Designer, should I have been given a copy of the Construction Phase Health and Safety Plan?

The Construction Phase Health and Safety Plan should be made available to all those who need to be familiar with it. If, as a Designer, you make regular visits to the site, you will need to have a good knowledge of the content of the Plan, as all persons will need to comply with aspects of the Plan.

Individual copies of the Plan may be issued by the Principal Contractor to the Project or Design Team. Alternatively, a copy may be made available at the Site Office.

If you are acting as a Contractor as well as a Designer, you will need to have a copy of the Plan.

All persons reporting to a construction site have duties to ensure their health and safety, and the Construction Phase Health and Safety Plan will contain Site Rules. All persons must comply with Site Rules, especially Designers as they represent the Client and must lead by example.

Health and safety management is a joint responsibility for everyone involved in a construction project and the more communication and co-operation there is between all parties, the greater the standards of safety achieved.

Legislation

Construction (Design and Management) Regulations 1994

- *Regulation 15*
- *Regulation 16*

Codes of Practice

Managing Health and Safety in Construction (HSG 224: ISBN 0 7176 2139 1)

As the Project Designer, what action should I take if I notice something inherently unsafe while I am on the construction site?

If you believe there is an 'imminent risk of serious personal injury', you must stop the activity from continuing if practical and safe to do so. Advise operatives of your concerns and advise them to suspend the activity until you have consulted with the Site Agent.

Inform the Site Agent of your observations, concerns and actions, and agree with him a renewed safe system of work. This may need you, as Designer, to adjust your design or sequence of construction so as to improve the safety situation.

If the activity you notice is unsafe but not inherently and immediately dangerous, report the matter as soon as possible to the Site Agent and request he take preventative action.

Remember, the Principal Contractor, by way of the Site Agent, has overall responsibility for the health and safety of the site.

Legislation

Construction (Design and Management) Regulations 1994

- *Regulation 13*
- *Regulation 16*

Construction (Health, Safety & Welfare) Regulations 1996
Health & Safety at Work Etc. Act 1974

Code of Practice

Managing Health and Safety in Construction (HSG 224: ISBN 0 7176 2139 1)

Case Study

The Planning Supervisor was making regular visits to a construction site where major roof refurbishment works were being carried out as required by the Client.

During an unannounced visit to the site, the Planning Supervisor noticed roofing workers working at heights in an inherently unsafe manner. Several operatives were straddling steel roofing trusses without safety harnesses or any fall arrest system or safety netting. One slip and they would have fallen in excess of 20 metres. The risk of falling was compounded by the fact that they were over-reaching to pull a temporary roof covering over the trusses.

It was difficult to stop the works immediately and the Planning Supervisor believed that the risk would be increased if he shouted at them to stop. He sought out the Site Agent and took him to view the system of work. The Site Agent stopped works immediately.

The Planning Supervisor requested a review of all Method Statements, Risk Assessments, Design Risk Assessments and, on behalf of the Client, severely reprimanded the Principal Contractor for failing to ensure that safe systems of work prevailed on the site. There were no excuses for the failure as the Principal Contractor had been provided with all the relevant safety information in the Pre-tender Health and Safety Plan, and the Client had also stipulated specific site safety rules regarding working at height to be included in the Construction Phase Health and Safety Plan.

15

The Planning Supervisor

As Planning Supervisor, do I have to check Method Statements?

No. Method Statements are written procedures that indicate how a job is to be done safely — they depict the 'safe system of work' which the Health and Safety at Work Etc. Act 1974 requires.

The Planning Supervisor is not responsible for site safety issues and Method Statements cover the details of how things will be done on site.

If requested by the Principal Contractor, you can give guidance on the adequacy of the Method Statement in relation to the site-specific risks that you have identified in the Pre-tender Health and Safety Plan. You have a duty under Regulation 14 to give 'adequate advice' to any Contractor in order to help him comply with his responsibilities to assess competency and resources in respect of appointing Designers to undertake a design. A Designer is anyone who draws, issues design detail and specifications (including articles and substances), etc. Therefore, interpreting and commenting on a Method Statement might be useful advice if the Contractor is designing a scheme for shop fitting, for instance.

Legislation

Construction (Design and Management) Regulations 1994

- *Regulation 14*
- *Regulation 15*

Code of Practice

Managing Health and Safety in Construction (HSG 224: ISBN 0 7176 2139 1)

As Planning Supervisor, do I have a legal duty to carry out site safety audits during the Construction Phase?

The CDM Regulations do not impose duties on the Planning Supervisor to carry out site safety audits, nor to be responsible for safety on the construction site.

The Regulations place no duty on anyone to monitor the effectiveness of the Construction Phase Health and Safety Plan, other than, of course, the Principal Contractor.

Clients and Planning Supervisors may enter into contractual arrangements whereby the Planning Supervisor provides additional services to the Client and site safety auditing is often one such service. The requirement is contractual and not legal (although should the Planning Supervisor fail to fulfil his obligation, a breach of contract law would be created) and falls outside of CDM.

Where such an agreement exists between the Client and the Planning Supervisor, it is advisable to inform the Principal Contractor so that he knows that the Planning Supervisor has the Client's authority to act on health and safety issues.

Legislation

Construction (Design and Management) Regulations 1994

- *Regulation 14*
- *Regulation 15*

Code of Practice

Managing Health and Safety in Construction (HSG 224: ISBN 0 7176 2139 1)

As Planning Supervisor, do I need to visit the site during construction works?

As it is often the case that design continues throughout a project, including the construction phase, the Planning Supervisor will have a continuing role during construction in ensuring that Designers co-operate with each other, address their duties under Regulation 13 and provide further relevant information to the Principal Contractor.

Also, where some Contractors act as Designers, the Planning Supervisor will need to ensure they fulfil their CDM duties.

As the continuing design happens on the construction site, it would be advisable for the Planning Supervisor to visit the site periodically during the construction phase to gather information on new design aspects, design revisions, etc.

Also, the Planning Supervisor needs to gather information for the Health and Safety File and this is often best done by regular visits to the site to relieve the Principal Contractor of such information.

It would make sense to build into the project plan a regular Design Team safety meeting, whereby issues raised by continuing designs can be co-ordinated, discussed and agreed between all Designers — the true spirit of CDM for *co-operation* between Design Team members. Such a meeting would be best undertaken on site prior to, or after, a regular site progress meeting.

Site visits by the Planning Supervisor may also assist the Principal Contractor in seeking advice on the competency of any Contractor he wishes to appoint with design responsibilities.

Legislation

Construction (Design and Management) Regulations 1994

● *Regulation 14*

Code of Practice

Managing Health and Safety in Construction (HSG 224: ISBN 0 7176 2139 1)

Case Study

During the major refurbishment and new extension of a department store, the Planning Supervisor implemented a series of Project Team safety co-ordination meetings. These meetings were scheduled every two weeks for the first two months of construction and were designed to enable a co-ordinated approach to be taken to design issues involving the Architect, Interior Designer, Structural Engineer, Building Services Consultants and other specialist Designers.

The idea behind the meeting was to discuss, in an open forum, any areas of design that could have health and safety implications for others, e.g. structural matters interacting with mechanical services, the shared use of lifting equipment, etc.

Minutes were taken from the meeting and circulated to the Project Team.

Designers felt they were co-operating with one another and that their designs were being co-ordinated.

16

The Principal Contractor

Do Method Statements/Risk Assessments have to be sent to the Planning Supervisor? Is it a legal requirement to do so?

No. There is no duty placed on the Planning Supervisor, under the CDM Regulations, to monitor site safety or to be involved in the development of the Construction Phase Health and Safety Plan.

There is no duty placed on the Client under CDM to monitor site safety or to check whether the Principal Contractor is following the Construction Phase Health and Safety Plan.

Therefore, there is nothing to be gained by the Principal Contractor sending Method Statements or Risk Assessments to the Planning Supervisor *unless* the Client has instructed the Planning Supervisor to assist the Principal Contractor in such matters by an agreement outside the duties required by CDM.

If the Method Statement contains the sequence of construction or similar information, it could be a useful document for inclusion in the Health and Safety File in case of future demolition of the structure and, in this instance, it would be appropriate to send the Method Statement to the Planning Supervisor.

Legislation

Construction (Design and Management) Regulations 1994

- *Regulation 14*
- *Regulation 15*
- *Regulation 16*

Code of Practice

Managing Health and Safety in Construction (HSG 224: ISBN 0 7176 2139 1)

Guidance

A Guide to Managing Health and Safety in Construction (HSE: ISBN 0 7176 07550)

Why should Method Statements/Risk Assessments be completed and when should they be done and for what type of work?

Method Statements are written procedures that outline how a job is to be done so as to ensure the safety of everyone involved with the job, including persons who are in the vicinity.

A Method Statement equates to a 'safe system of work' which is required under the Health and Safety at Work Etc. Act 1974.

Risk Assessments are required under the Management of Health and Safety at Work Regulations 1999 and all employers are required to assess the risks to workers and any others who may be affected by their undertaking.

A Risk Assessment identifies hazards present, evaluates the risks involved and identifies control measures necessary to eliminate or minimise the risks of injury or ill-health.

A Method Statement can be used as the control measure needed to eliminate or minimise the risks involved in carrying out the job.

As Principal Contractor you should carry out Risk Assessments for all work activities which you require your *employees* to do, i.e. your own employed tradesmen.

Also, as Principal Contractor, you should carry out Risk Assessments for all those work activities which involve all operatives on site, i.e. communal activities such as access routes to places of work, delivery of materials, plant and equipment, etc.

As Principal Contractor you should receive risk assessments from all the other Contractors, Sub-contractors and self-employed tradesmen working on the site. These will tell you what the hazards associated with their tasks are, e.g. noise from drilling equipment, and will include details of how the risks from the hazards, e.g. noise-induced hearing loss, can be eliminated or reduced.

When you have reviewed each of the Contractor/Sub-contractor Risk Assessments you must consider whether, as Principal Contractor, you need to do anything else to protect other workers in the area, i.e. forbid certain work activities in certain areas, etc. If so, you will need to do an additional Risk Assessment which identifies how, as Principal Contractor, you are going to manage and control the combined risks of several Contractors.

Risk Assessments need only identify *significant* risks involved in carrying out a work activity. Routine risks and everyday risks, such as crossing the road to get to the employee car park, need not be included.

Where anything unusual or uncommon is to be undertaken on the site, a Risk Assessment will be essential. Where works involve significant hazards, e.g. working in confined spaces, working at heights, working with harmful substances, then Risk Assessments are legally required and the control measures identified could be incorporated into a Method Statement which operatives are required to follow.

Legislation

Construction (Design and Management) Regulations 1994

- *Regulation 15*
- *Regulation 16*

  Management of Health & Safety at Work Regulations 1999

- *Regulation 3*

Code of Practice

Managing Health and Safety in Construction (HSG 224: ISBN 0 7176 2139 1)

Guidance

A Guide to Managing Health and Safety in Construction (HSE: ISBN 0 7176 07550)

Can generic Risk Assessments be used as the basis of the Health and Safety Plan?

Yes, but they may not be sufficient for you to demonstrate that you have done everything 'reasonably practicable' to ensure the health and safety of all persons at work carrying out construction works.

Generic Risk Assessments, i.e. those that cover the general work activities such as bricklaying, form the basis of identifying hazards and risks associated with the job. Provided you develop the generic Risk Assessment to include any site-specific hazard, e.g. carrying out brickwork adjacent to a deep water course, and the additional control measures you intend to adopt, you will have sufficient information to ensure operatives work safely.

When reviewing a Construction Health and Safety Plan the HSE Inspector will not be satisfied with a Plan that contains only general information, no matter how thick and impressive the Plan looks. Often, a much thinner and more accurate site-specific Plan will gain praise from the Inspector. They will look for information proportional to the project risks — too much information is confusing and often of little value.

Legislation

Construction (Design and Management) Regulations 1994

● *Regulation 15*

Case Study

The Principal Contractor was responsible for ensuring the delivery of materials to site. The delivery area incorporated the rear access road which was shared by a neighbouring retail premises. There were hazards to both the site operatives and adjoining tenants from the delivery vehicles and the off loading of materials. Hazards included moving vehicles, restricted access to the roadway for emergency vehicles, off-loading materials from the lorries, dust, noise, and falling objects. The risks from the hazards included being knocked over, being hit by materials, noise-induced hearing loss, breathing in dust and exhaust fumes, etc.

The Principal Contractor formulated the Risk Assessment, identifying the above as the hazards and risks, and determining the control measures needed to eliminate or minimise the risks. These included having a banksman to guide in the delivery vehicles, setting specific delivery times, liasing with the adjoining tenants, providing lifting devices, requiring engines to be switched off during delivery, avoiding reversing vehicles wherever possible, etc. (See Appendix 16 for the Risk Assessments.)

The Principal Contractor then prepared a short Method Statement which was given to the Site Foreman to follow when deliveries occurred. (See Appendix 17 for the Method Statement.)

The preparation of this Risk Assessment and Method Statement was the Principal Contractor's responsibility because he had overall management control of these activities and could co-ordinate everyone else's deliveries to site.

Code of Practice

Managing Health and Safety in Construction (HSG 224: ISBN 0 7176 2139 1)

Guidance

A Guide to Managing Health and Safety in Construction (HSE: ISBN 0 7176 07550)

What other requirements does the Principal Contractor have to comply with in respect of CDM?

In addition to developing the Construction Phase Health and Safety Plan, the Principal Contractor has specific duties laid down in Regulation 16 of the CDM Regulations.

These include:

- ensuring co-operation between all Contractors on the site or on adjacent sites where there is an overlap, e.g. shared access routes
- ensuring that all Contractors and all employees work in connection with the rules contained in the Health and Safety Plan
- ensuring that only authorised persons are allowed into the premises where construction works are being carried out
- ensuring that the HSE notification of Form F10 is displayed, is in a readable condition and is in a position where anyone involved in the construction works can read it
- providing the Planning Supervisor with information, particularly if that information would be necessary for inclusion in the Health and Safety File
- giving reasonable direction to any Contractor, so far as is necessary, to enable the Principal Contractor to comply with his duties
- ensuring that the Safety Rules contained in the Health and Safety Plan are in writing and are brought to the attention of persons who may be affected by them.

In order to be able to ensure co-operation between all Contractors, it is necessary to have an understanding of Regulations 11 and 12 of the Management of Health and Safety at Work Regulations 1999. These Regulations require employers and the self-employed to co-ordinate their activities, co-operate with each other and to share information to help each other comply with their statutory duties.

For instance, to be effective, Risk Assessments will need to cover the workplace as a whole and it will be the Principal Contractor's duty to co-ordinate these activities. Information must be provided by all employers/Contractors so as to enable the Principal Contractor to co-ordinate activities.

Another important aspect of co-ordination and co-operation relates to the use of work equipment and tools that are shared by all Contractors on the site. The Principal Contractor may assume responsibility for provision, maintenance and testing of all common equipment, e.g. lifting devices, or he may pass the responsibility onto another Contractor. It does not matter *who* does it as long as someone assumes responsibility and everyone else knows who that person is.

The Principal Contractor will need to request the names of all the people, Contractors, Clients, and the Design Team, etc. who wish to visit the site as 'authorised persons'. The Principal Contractor may authorise them to enter all or part of the site. The Principal Contractor should adopt a formal signing in procedure which all persons should follow. Unauthorised visitors should be accompanied around the site by a trained operative.

Under Regulation 17 of CDM, as Principal Contractor you have responsibility for ensuring that every Contractor is provided with comprehensive information on the risks to health and safety to all employees and others on the site.

In addition, you must ensure that every employer carries out suitable training for all employees, relative to the works involved and, also, that they provide information relating to health and safety issues.

'Comprehensive' information need not just be in writing — it could be diagrams, or drawings, or it could be information in languages other than English.

The most appropriate way to ensure information is available is to include it in the Health and Safety Plan.

Under Regulation 18 of CDM, as Principal Contractor you must ensure that there are procedures in place for any employee or self-employed person to discuss health and safety issues, and that there are arrangements for co-ordinating the views of others in respect of health and safety issues.

Depending on the size of the project, all that may be required will be an item for health and safety on a site meeting agenda and a formal process whereby someone can raise health and safety concerns without fear of reprisals.

Legislation

Construction (Design and Management) Regulations 1994

- *Regulation 15*
- *Regulation 16*
- *Regulation 17*
- *Regulation 18*

Code of Practice

Managing Health and Safety in Construction (HSG 224: ISBN 0 7176 2139 1)

What other legislation does the Principal Contractor have to comply with in respect of health and safety?

The CDM Regulations are only one set of Regulations governing safety which are applicable to construction sites.

Other applicable health and safety legislation include:

- Health & Safety at Work Etc. Act 1974
- Health & Safety (First Aid) Regulations 1981

- Control of Asbestos at Work Regulations 1987
- Noise at Work Regulations 1989
- Electricity at Work Regulations 1989
- Management of Health & Safety at Work Regulations 1999
- Provision and Use of Work Equipment Regulations 1998
- Personal Protective Equipment Regulations 1992
- Manual Handling Operations Regulations 1992
- Control of Substances Hazardous to Health Regulations 1999
- Reporting of Injuries, Diseases and Dangerous Occurrences Regulations 1995
- Construction (Health, Safety & Welfare) Regulations 1996
- The Fire Precautions (Places of Work) Regulations 1997 (amended)
- Confined Space Regulations 1997
- The Lifting Operations and Lifting Equipment Regulations 1998
- Control of Lead at Work Regulations 1998
- Contruction (Head Protection) Regulations 1989

Additional legislation that covers specific, specialist topics, e.g. Ionising Radiation Regulations 1985 and Control of Lead at Work Regulations 1998, may also be applicable to the works on site.

What does the Principal Contractor have to provide regarding training for operatives on site?

The CDM Regulations do not actually require the Principal Contractor to provide training (other than to his own employees) to operatives on site but to ensure that every Contractor is provided with comprehensible information on the risks to health and safety from work activities on the site.

Comprehensive information is information which is understood by everyone. It is meaningless to issue complex Site Rules and Risk Assessments if the understanding of written English is poor. Verbal instructions, diagrams, etc. may be more comprehensible.

The Principal Contractor should also ensure that every Contractor who is an employer provides any of his employees with information, instruction and training as required by the Management of Health and Safety at Work Regulations 1999.

Site induction training is considered to be the responsibility of the Principal Contractor and the information given should include:

- Site Rules
- emergency procedures
- fire safety
- accident procedures
- permit to work systems
- site security
- welfare facilities on site
- first aid facilities
- management of health and safety on the site.

All the above information should be included in the Construction Phase Health and Safety Plan and a copy of the Plan should be given to the Site Foreman of every Contractor on the site.

Whether the Principal Contractor or each individual Contractor carries out site induction training, it is essential that written records of the training are kept and regularly reviewed and updated.

The Principal Contractor may require all Contractors to provide evidence of competency in the various trades and will be entitled to request training certificates for trades such as mobile equipment driving, fork lift truck driving, gas fitting works, etc.

All such documentation should be kept readily available by the Principal Contractor and is best kept appended to the Construction Phase Health and Safety Plan.

The Health and Safety Plan should set out what level of training site operatives are expected to have, who is to have provided it, how often and to what standard.

The Principal Contractor's role in respect of training is a co-ordination role unless he is an employer of his own workforce when the requirements of health and safety training and the provision of information will apply equally to the Principal Contractor as to others.

Legislation

Construction (Design and Management) Regulations 1994

● *Regulation 17*

Management of Health & Safety at Work Regulations 1999

● *Regulation 10*
● *Regulation 13*

Code of Practice

Managing Health and Safety in Construction (HSG 224: ISBN 0 7176 2139 1)

Guidance

A Guide to Managing Health and Safety in Construction (HSE: ISBN 0 7176 07550)

The Client has appointed several 'Client Direct' appointments who are employed by the Client and required to access the site to undertake works. Are they exempt from complying with CDM?

No. As Principal Contractor you have absolute responsibility for site safety issues and can specify these in the Site Rules included in the Construction Phase Health and Safety Plan.

Even if the 'Client Direct' is not a 'Contractor' under the Regulations, they will either be employers or employees and, as such, have legal duties under the Management of Health & Safety at Work Regulations 1999 to comply with the requirements of the Principal Contractor.

Contractors are defined in Regulation 2 (1) of CDM as:

any person who carries on a trade, business or other undertaking (whether for profit or not) in connection with which he:

(a) undertakes to or does carry out or manage construction work,
(b) arranges for any person at work under his control (including, where he is an employer, any employee of his) to carry out or manage construction work.

Construction work includes fitting out, commissioning, alteration, conversion, etc.

Regulation 19 (2) of CDM applies to all *employers* and states that they must not cause or permit any employee to work on construction work unless the employer has been provided with relevant information, namely the name of the Planning Supervisor and Principal Contractor and the contents of the Health and Safety Plan. In any event, Regulations 11 and 12 of the Management of Health & Safety at Work Regulations 1999 apply, i.e. co-operation of a multi-occupied site and the appointment of a controlling employer for the site. Information has to be shared regarding Risk Assessments, as required under Regulation 10 of the Management of Health & Safety at Work Regulations 1999.

The Principal Contractor has a duty under Regulation 16 of CDM to ensure that every *employee* at work in connection with the project complies with any rules contained in the Health and Safety Plan. If the Health and Safety Plan contains a rule which states that all Client Direct appointments and any others conducting a trade, business or undertaking, shall provide Method Statements/Risk Assessments to the Principal Contractor prior to commencing work, they must legally comply with the rule.

Legislation

Construction (Design and Management) Regulations 1994

- *Regulation 2*
- *Regulation 15*

- *Regulation 16*
- *Regulation 19*

Management of Health & Safety at Work Regulations 1999

- *Regulation 10*
- *Regulation 11*
- *Regulation 12*

Code of Practice

Managing Health and Safety in Construction (HSG 224: ISBN 0 7176 2139 1)

Guidance

A Guide to Managing Health and Safety in Construction (HSE: ISBN 0 7176 07550)

What actions can the Principal Contractor take where either Contractors or Client Direct appointments fail to comply with the Site Rules, Health and Safety Plan or CDM requirements?

Remove them from site — although this is probably easier said than done.

Write to the employer of the Contractors/Client Direct and advise them that they are in breach of their duties under CDM Regulations and other health and safety legislation and unless they start complying they will be removed from site, incurring any contractual penalties.

Often non-compliance with a requirement is due to fear or ignorance. Perhaps they do not know how to conduct Risk Assessments. If this is the case, provide information and guidance.

Review your procedures for assessing competency of Contractors. Remember the duty to ensure competency of Contractors rests with *any person*, including Principal Contractors who let subsidiary work packages to Sub-contractors. Did you know the Contractor could not provide Risk Assessments? If so, why appoint them.

Consider whether you are asking the Contractor to provide more information than is justifiable. Risk Assessments and Method Statements need to be relevant and cover *significant* risks. Requesting meaningless paperwork from Contractors merely compounds their reluctance to produce any.

Ask the Planning Supervisor to help encourage the Contractor/ Client Direct to comply with their statutory duties. The Planning Supervisor could give advice to the Client that the Contractor is not competent and recommend that the Client moves to formally dismiss the Contractor.

Ask the local HSE Inspector for guidance. If the site is complying with CDM then there is nothing to fear in seeking advice from an Inspector on how to improve your health and safety management procedures, e.g. improving Contractor compliance.

De-list the Contractor/Client Direct from your approved list.

Whatever steps you take, do not allow the breach of safety management procedures to go unrecorded. Keep detailed records of what actions you took to ensure compliance with Site Rules, who you spoke to, when, how often, etc. Make sure you have given them the information they could reasonably expect to have regarding the site works, e.g. Health and Safety Plan.

Legislation

Construction (Design and Management) Regulations 1994

- *Regulation 15*
- *Regulation 16*
- *Regulation 19*

Code of Practice

Managing Health and Safety in Construction (HSG 224: ISBN 0 7176 2139 1)

What happens if the Principal Contractor does not fulfil his responsibilities under CDM?

As Principal Contractor, you will be in breach of your duties under Regulation 16 and possibly Regulation 15 of CDM (if you do not have a suitable and sufficient Construction Phase Health and Safety Plan) and could be prosecuted by the HSE.

Also, contraventions of Regulations 17 and 18 are offences carrying criminal charges.

If you fail to prevent unauthorised persons from entering the site you are committing a criminal offence. In addition, if that unauthorised person has an accident and decides to sue the Principal Contractor in the Civil Courts, the fact that you have been charged with an offence under Regulation 16 (1) will be 'prima facie' evidence of guilt in the civil action.

The HSE will prosecute Principal Contractors who fail to discharge their CDM duties effectively.

Prosecutions are taken either in the Magistrates' Court or in the Crown Court, and fines have the potential to be unlimited.

Legislation

Construction (Design and Management) Regulations 1994

- *Regulation 15*
- *Regulation 16*
- *Regulation 17*
- *Regulation 18*

Code of Practice

Managing Health and Safety in Construction (HSG 224: ISBN 0 7176 2139 1)

Guidance

A Guide to Managing Health and Safety in Construction (HSE: ISBN 0 7176 07550)

What notices under CDM must the Principal Contractor display on site?

The Principal Contractor must ensure that a copy of the Notification of Project (Form F10), as sent to the HSE by the Planning Supervisor, is displayed on the site and that it remains legible and can be read by those working on the site.

The Notice can be displayed in the Site Office but this may restrict the number of operatives who could easily refer to it. An acceptable place to display the Form F10 would be in the welfare or messing facilities where it would be readily available to all operatives. A copy could be kept in the Site Office or with the Construction Phase Health and Safety Plan.

The location of the Form F10 Notice needs to be brought to the attention of all Contractors working on the site and the easiest way to do this is to inform them during the site induction training.

Legislation

Construction (Design and Management) Regulations 1994

- *Regulation 16*

Code of Practice

Managing Health and Safety in Construction (HSG 224: ISBN 0 7176 2139 1)

Is the Principal Contractor responsible for providing welfare facilities on the construction site?

Usually, yes. The Construction (Health, Safety & Welfare) Regulations 1996 state that the person in control of a construction site is responsible for seeing that welfare facilities are provided and maintained to a standard as specified in the Regulations, e.g. number of facilities, sanitary accommodation, cleanliness, etc.

Where the CDM Regulations apply, this duty is normally placed on the Principal Contractor. The Pre-tender Health and Safety Plan should contain specific details as to who is responsible and whether the Client will be providing shared accommodation, etc.

The Principal Contractor cannot require Contractors to provide their own welfare facilities and must make facilities available to all contractors on the site.

Legislation

Construction (Design and Management) Regulations 1994

- *Regulation 15*
- *Regulation 16*

Construction (Health, Safety & Welfare) Regulations 1996

- *Regulation 22*
- *Schedule 6*

What type of welfare facilities must be provided by the Principal Contractor?

Regulation 22 of the Construction (Health, Safety & Welfare) Regulations 1996 sets out the requirements for the provision of welfare facilities. The 'person in control of the site' must comply with the duty to provide suitable and sufficient welfare facilities and this will be determined by a Risk Assessment.

Schedule 6 of the Regulations sets out the principles to be observed and these can be summarised as follows.

- Toilets:
  - no numbers are specified but they should be suitable and sufficient for the number of operatives on site — a guide table is produced in Appendix 18
  - adequate lighting and ventilation must be provided
  - sanitary accommodation must be kept clean
  - separate male and female accommodation is not required if each water closet is in a separate room with a door which can be locked from the inside.
- Washing facilities:
  - washing facilities include wash hand-basins and, if necessary due to the type of work, showers
  - facilities should be in the immediate vicinity of sanitary accommodation and reasonably accessible throughout the site
  - clean hot and cold, or warm water, must be provided, preferably as running water
  - soap or other hand-cleaning chemicals must be provided, together with hand-drying facilities
  - facilities should be well lit and ventilated, and kept clean
  - unless washing facilities are provided in individual cubicles, there shall be male and female facilities unless they are used only for washing hands, face and forearms.
- Drinking water:
  - a clean, wholesome supply of water for drinking shall be provided in readily accessible locations
  - drinking water supplies must be labelled or signed as suitable for consumption
  - drinking vessels shall be provided if the water is not from a drinking fountain.
- Accommodation for clothing:
  - facilities need to be made available for everyday clothes not worn on the site and for special clothing worn at work, but not taken home

- ○ drying facilities have to be provided for clothing
- ○ changing facilities must be provided where specialised clothing is required to be worn.
- Rest facilities:
  - ○ suitable and sufficient rest facilities shall be provided, which include areas for eating and preparing meals
  - ○ consideration must be given to protecting non-smokers from the harmful effects of tobacco smoke
  - ○ where necessary, facilities for pregnant or nursing mothers must be provided.

Legislation

Construction (Health, Safety & Welfare) Regulations 1996

- *Regulation 22*
- *Schedule 6*

What training must be provided by the Principal Contractor?

The CDM Regulations do not specifically require the Principal Contractor to carry out training for persons other than his own employees.

The Principal Contractor is responsible for ensuring that all Contractors working on the site are given comprehensible information about the risks they are likely to face during their work on site.

In addition, the Principal Contractor must ensure that Contractors provide their employees with relevant training which covers new or increased risks from working on the project.

Notwithstanding the above, the Principal Contractor may be required to carry out induction training as a requirement of the Client and such a 'Site Rule' would have been included in the Pre-tender Health and Safety plan and further developed by the

Principal Contractor in the Construction Phase Health and Safety Plan.

Induction training arranged by the Principal Contractor may be the simplest way for the Principal Contractor to discharge his duties in respect of making information available to all Contractors. An organised, planned induction programme would give the Principal Contractor a mechanism to record attendees and to keep training records. In the event of any accident or incident, the Principal Contractor would have attendance records to show that he had discharged his duties regarding the sharing of information relevant to health and safety risks comprehensively.

Legislation

Construction (Design and Management) Regulations 1994

● *Regulation 18*

Code of Practice

Managing Health and Safety in Construction (HSG 224: ISBN 0 7176 2139 1)

What subjects would be appropriate to include in induction training organised by the Principal Contractor?

The duty of the Principal Contractor is to convey information on risks relating to the carrying out of construction works within the designated site. One of the most effective ways to communicate information is by way of a structured training programme. Subjects to cover in induction training would be:

● outline of the project — who's who, e.g. Client, Design Team, etc.

- statement on health and safety and commitment of Senior Management to high standards of health and safety
- site-specific risks, e.g.:
  - ○ access routes
  - ○ contaminated land
  - ○ overhead power cables
  - ○ underground services
  - ○ proximity of water
  - ○ unstable buildings
  - ○ hazardous materials, e.g. asbestos
- site-specific control measures for identified risks
- Site Rules
- welfare facilities available, location maintenance and cleaning provision, etc.
- first aid facilities
- accident and near miss reporting procedures
- emergency procedures, e.g.:
  - ○ fire evacuation
  - ○ raising the fire alarm
  - ○ name and address of emergency services
  - ○ assembly point
  - ○ fire marshals/wardens
  - ○ building collapse
  - ○ flood, chemical escape and gas escapes
  - ○ release of hazardous substances, such as asbestos
- responsible persons
- requirements for protective equipment and clothing, e.g.:
  - ○ use of hard hats
  - ○ use of safety footwear
  - ○ use of ear defenders
- general site safety controls, e.g.:
  - ○ permit to work
  - ○ permit to enter
  - ○ use of banksmen
- arrangements for communicating with all the workforce in respect of health and safety, e.g.:

○ weekly site safety meetings
○ notice board
○ display of safety notices
○ use of other aids, such as visual aids to assist those with language difficulties
● names of safety representatives, competent persons, etc.
● site security and access procedures.

All of the above information should be available in the Construction Phase Health and Safety Plan and key details should be displayed on an information board at the entrance to the site or in the messing facilities.

Legislation

Construction (Design and Management) Regulations 1994

● *Regulation 15*
● *Regulation 16*
● *Regulation 17*
● *Regulation 18*
● *Regulation 19*

Code of Practice

Managing Health and Safety in Construction (HSG 224: ISBN 0 7176 2139 1)

Case Study

A new shopping centre was being constructed for a consortium of developers. The developers nominated the main developer as the Client under the CDM Regulations and, as Client, the main developer appointed a Management Contractor to oversee the entire construction works. The Management Contractor was designated Principal Contractor even though they were not undertaking any actual construction works but because they managed the construction process they met the qualification requirement of CDM for a Principal Contractor.

The Client required the Principal Contractor to have overall responsibility for the site and although each tenant shop fit-out had a Main Contractor, only the Management Contractor was designated Principal Contractor.

The Client imposed a duty on the Principal Contractor to carry out induction training for *all* persons entering the site.

The Principal Contractor set up a separate training room within his Site Office compound and by way of a strict security control point, all persons entering the site for the first time had to report to the training office for induction.

Each induction programme ran for 30 minutes and three sessions were undertaken each day — two in the morning and one in the early afternoon. If persons wanted to gain access to the site at other times, they had to wait until the next induction session.

Every person going through the induction process was registered and when they had completed the course, they signed a declaration to that effect. These records were kept centrally by the Management Contractor.

Each attendee received a photo ID card, which indicated that they had been inducted and when. On the reverse of the ID card were the basic emergency rules of the site.

Each individual Main Contractor undertaking their own Client's shop fit-out was required to provide additional training to operatives about the specific hazards and risks found on the site.

Each Main Contractor had to regularly provide information to the Principal Contractor on any health and safety issue in their site which could affect the safety of the whole site, e.g. LPG storage. The Principal Contractor then ensured this information was added to its induction training programme.

17

Contractors

What are the main duties of Contractors under the CDM Regulations?

Contractors are given specific duties under Regulation 19 of CDM as follows:

- co-operate with the Principal Contractor in order that they both comply with their legal duties under *all* applicable legislation
- provide the Principal Contractor with information, including, if necessary, Risk Assessments, on any activity, material, process or task which might affect the health and safety of any person at work carrying on construction works, or of any person who may be affected or which might cause the Principal Contractor to review health and safety across the site
- comply with any directions the Principal Contractor gives in relation to Site Rules or any other health and safety matter which the Principal Contractor has a duty to fulfil
- comply with the rules contained in the Health and Safety Plan
- provide information promptly to the Principal Contractor in relation to accidents, diseases or dangerous occurrences, including any fatalities, which the Contractor would need to report under the Reporting of Injuries, Diseases and Dangerous Occurrences Regulations 1985.
- provide information to the Principal Contractor on any matter which it might be reasonable to assume the Principal Contractor will need to pass on to the Planning Supervisor for the Health and Safety File.

In addition to the above, if the Contractor is an employer or a self-employed person, they shall not start any construction works until they have been provided with the nature of the Planning Supervisor and the Principal Contractor, i.e. have been given, or have seen, a copy of Form F10.

All contractors must have relevant parts of the Construction Phase Health and Safety Plan as relates to the work they will carry out on the site.

Legislation

Construction (Design and Management) Regulations 1994

● *Regulation 19*

Code of Practice

Managing Health and Safety in Construction (HSG 224: ISBN 0 7176 2139 1)

What responsibilities do Contractors have for on-site training of their operatives?

Where Contractors are employers they have general duties under health and safety legislation to ensure that their employees receive suitable and sufficient training, or information, instruction and training.

A general duty for training employees is contained in Regulation 13 of the Management of Health and Safety at Work Regulations 1999, especially where they are likely to face new or increased risks within the work environment.

The Principal Contractor has a duty under CDM to ensure that Contractors provide training to their employees and could include these requirements in the Construction Phase Health and Safety Plan.

Principal Contractors may require evidence from Contractors of such training in, for example, the form of training records, copies of certificates, etc.

Contractors must ensure that they address any specific training needs relative to the site activities and, in particular, they must cover topics with which their employees may not normally be familiar.

Legislation

Construction (Design and Management) Regulations 1994

● *Regulation 19*

Managing Health & Safety at Work Regulations 1999

● *Regulation 13*

Code of Practice

Managing Health and Safety in Construction (HSG 224: ISBN 0 7176 2139 1)
Management of Health & Safety at Work (ACOP L21)

The Principal Contractor has not organised induction training. What should Contractors do?

Good health and safety starts with communication and co-operation, so the first step to take is to discuss the matter with the Principal Contractor.

Review the Construction Phase Health and Safety Plan to see how the process of induction training is to be implemented and inform the Principal Contractor if there seems to be a discrepancy.

Under Regulation 18 CDM, the Principal Contractor must ensure that there is a mechanism for employees and the self-employed at work on the construction site to discuss and offer advice in respect of health and safety.

Case Study

A Contractor was appointed by the Principal Contractor to provide specialised finishes to internal walls and ceilings. The Principal Contractor had arranged for all works at height to be carried out from mobile elevating work platforms for safety reasons.

The specialist Contractor's operatives were not familiar with using these devices as their work usually involved using mobile tower scaffolds.

The Principal Contractor gave the Contractor's operatives induction training regarding the general hazards on the site, emergency procedures, etc., and explained the management procedures for commonly used equipment, provided by the Principal Contractor.

Prior to allowing works to commence, the Contracts Manager of the specialist Contractor arranged for his operatives to receive additional training on the safe use of mobile elevating work platforms.

Failure to have an appropriate induction training programme will affect the health and safety of the site and its operatives. The Principal Contractor has to *ensure* that Contractors have provided their employees with information about risks, control measures and emergency procedures.

If the Principal Contractor still fails to fulfil his legal duties, the next step is to seek advice from the Planning Supervisor regarding the competency of the Principal Contractor. The Planning Supervisor has a duty to provide advice to any Contractor with a view to them complying with their duties in competency and resources and, in turn, if information is made available to the Planning Supervisor which questions the competency of the Principal Contractor, the Planning Supervisor will have a duty to inform the Client.

Contractors are entitled to receive parts of the Construction Phase Health and Safety Plan which directly affect them and this would include information on welfare facilities, fire precautions, emergency planning, accident management, site security, etc. If this information is made available to the Contractors, they should be able to organise their own induction training rather than leave their operatives without it.

In some circumstances, the Principal Contractor may provide the relevant information to the Contractor's Site Foreman for them to give suitable 'toolbox talks' on site induction information.

Contractors must remember that the duty to ensure that their employees are adequately trained rests with them as employers and that this duty cannot be delegated to someone else.

Legislation

Construction (Design and Management) Regulations 1994

- *Regulation 18*
- *Regulation 19*

Management of Health & Safety at Work Regulations 1999

- *Regulation 13*

Code of Practice

Managing Health and Safety in Construction (HSG 224: ISBN 0 7176 2139 1)

Do Contractors have to provide Risk Assessments to the Principal Contractor?

The Principal Contractor has a duty to co-ordinate health and safety across the construction site and, in particular, must address hazards and risks which affect all operatives on the site, no matter who is their employer.

Under Regulation 19 a Contractor must provide relevant information to the Principal Contractor on any activity which might affect the safety of operatives or others working on or resorting to the site. Relevant information includes any part of a Risk Assessment made under the general provisions of the Management of Health & Safety at Work Regulations 1999.

Principal Contractors should not really require Risk Assessments for tasks which only affect the Contractor's operatives but, often, in order to ensure that a culture of health and safety pervades the site, the Principal Contractor may include a Site Rule which states that Risk Assessments for all activities must be provided to them. Contractors have a duty to comply with Site Rules.

Legislation

Construction (Design and Management) Regulations 1994

● *Regulation 19*

Code of Practice

Managing Health and Safety in Construction (HSG 224: ISBN 0 7176 2139 1)

18

Practical on-site initiatives

What are some of the practical safety initiatives which I can introduce to the construction project in my role as Principal Contractor?

Site safety does not stop with compliance of the CDM Regulations 1994. Legislation really only sets minimum standards to be achieved and good safety management endeavours to achieve higher standards. Good safety management has been proved to have positive benefits to employers, Contractors, Clients and employees, and, ultimately, reduces costs due to fewer accidents, incidents, downtime, stoppages, investigations, loss and damage to property and equipment, etc.

In order to encourage high standards of safety on construction sites, the HSE launched, during summer 2000, a campaign known as 'Working Well Together'.

This campaign encourages all those involved in a construction project to work together to reduce hazards and risks, and to improve overall standards of health and safety in construction.

The following pages outline some of the initiatives that have been, or can be, introduced during a construction project.

Preventing falls from heights

The Principal Contractor undertook the following actions:

- influenced Designers to schedule permanent access structures, e.g. staircases early in the project

- provided communal mobile tower scaffolds for use by all Contractors and assumed responsibility for daily checking and remedial repairs by competent persons
- provided full edge protection to all drops more than two metres
- included within the Site Rules procedures for safe working at heights
- introduced a Permit to Work System for all work to be undertaken above two metres
- required all Contractors to provide Risk Assessments and a work plan for all activities they proposed to undertake above two metres
- required all Contractors to undertake toolbox talks on working at heights, the hazards, risks and controls necessary, and required evidence from each Contractor of such training or instruction
- provided a site audit function to check regularly on activity.

Preventing slips, trips and falls

The Principal Contractor introduced the following:

- information on slips, trips and falls, types of injury sustained, etc., included with site induction training
- clearer emphasis within Site Safety Rules on good housekeeping, trailing cables, etc.
- provision of adequate numbers of transformers, etc., in the location near to where power tools are to be used
- regular site safety inspections
- employed a site labourer, dedicated to clearing the site of debris, etc.
- adequate provision for skips, etc., on site for containing waste materials, etc.
- regular maintenance of floor surfaces, infilling of holes, etc.
- specific toolbox talks with electricians so that they did not leave floor box recesses unguarded
- provision of good, overall site lighting and, where necessary, appropriate task lighting
- assessment of operative's footwear.

Improvements in manual handling

The Principal Contractor introduced the following:

- mechanical lifting devices available to all Contractors on the site, co-ordinated by the Principal Contractor, and maintained and certified by him as necessary
- overall assessment of what materials were needed to be delivered to the site, where they needed to be used, where they could be stored, etc. — this entailed requesting from all Contractors plans of work and scheduled deliveries of materials, etc.
- inclusion within the site induction training of a section on manual handling, hazards and risks, and aspects of manual handling that have been identified within the site, using a training video
- requirement for all Contractors to provide Risk Assessments and Method Statements for manual handling activities
- alterations to specifications of materials so that smaller and less heavy sizes were delivered to site
- poster campaign around the site.

Painting and decorating

The Principal Contractor was aware that the majority of painters and decorators on site were small companies or self-employed individuals. Their general awareness of health and safety was poor and other trades were complaining to the Site Agent. The Principal Contractor decided to implement an awareness campaign on health and safety for the painters and decorators and introduced the following:

- toolbox talks by the Principal Contractor's Site Safety Officer on:
  - working at heights
  - working with hazardous substances
  - working with power tools
  - working in close proximity to other trades and people
  - housekeeping

- requirements for Method Statements and Risk Assessments for all work activity
- easy access to mobile tower scaffolds provided by the Principal Contractor
- leaflet campaign on contact dermatitis of hands and arms
- early morning work co-ordination meetings to agree who would be working where, what the hazards would be, etc.

Improving health and safety awareness of Site Foremen and Supervisors

The Principal Contractor included a section in the Construction Phase Health and Safety to improve health and safety awareness of all Contractor and Sub-contractor Site Foremen and Supervisors. During the tendering process, each Contractor had to agree to sign up and commit to the Site Foreman initiative.

The Principal Contractor included a section in the Construction Phase Health and Safety to improve health and safety awareness of all Contractor and Sub-contractor Foreman and Supervisors. During the tendering process, each Contractor had to agree to sign up and commit to the Site Foreman initiative.

The Principal Contractor then introduced the following:

- special training sessions for all Site Foremen on the roles and responsibilities for managing health and safety
- regular site safety inspections carried out with each Site Foreman
- a safety review meeting held weekly and attended by all Site Foremen and Supervisors
- accident prevention campaign that highlighted a safety topic every month and reviewed incidents and accidents
- guidance and best practice booklets produced by the Principal Contractor's own Safety Department for distribution to each Site Foreman
- site-specific safety audit checklists that each Site Foreman was required to complete and return to the Principal Contractor

- introduction of a 'Safety Default Notice' system that recorded poor standards of health and safety against each Contractor.

Site safety campaign

The Client on a major retail store development project was the instigator of a site safety campaign which was operated by the Principal Contractor on the Client's behalf. The best performing Contractor in respect of health and safety was awarded a monetary sum for donation to a charity of their choice.

The Principal Contractor decided that the award should be given to the Contractor who had made the most and greatest contribution to overall site safety. This involved not only ensuring that their own operatives were highly safety conscious, but that they also conducted their undertaking in such a way that the safety of others was improved.

The Principal Contractor arranged information meetings with all the Contractors on site and set out clearly the performance criteria expected.

Assessments would be made on the following:

- frequency and efficiency of toolbox talks
- practical, working knowledge of the operatives on site of general health and safety principles
- quality and effectiveness of Method Statements and Risk Assessments
- co-operation and co-ordination of work with other Contractors
- general commitment to health and safety, demonstrated by pro-active attendance at the weekly site safety meeting.

The Principal Contractor provided the services of the on-site Safety Officer to any Contractor who wished to have extra assistance in upgrading their health and safety practices. The Principal Contractor provided all Contractors with a basic training pack for toolbox talks and attended many as an observer. Contractors were required to provide evidence of toolbox talks and individual operatives were interviewed to establish their learning outcomes.

The campaign ran for a three-month period and the Principal Contractor and the Client, assisted by the Planning Supervisor, assessed all information, accident records, etc., and decided on an outright winner.

A presentation award ceremony was arranged in the site canteen and the Client's Director presented a cheque for £500 to the successful Contractor. In turn, they presented a cheque to a children's disability charity.

Similarly, on a major pharmaceutical company's research and development campus construction site, the Managing Contractor, as Principal Contractor, implemented an 'Accident Free Working Hours' campaign and set an objective to reach 1 million working hours free of any major accident or incident. The Site Safety Officer ran numerous campaigns on the site on safety topics, supported by poster campaigns, training, site audits, feedback to Contractors, etc. When milestones of accident free working hours were met, all operatives on the site were awarded some tokens of achievement, such as t-shirts, mugs, kit bags, etc. When a major milestone, such as 500,000 accident free working hours, was achieved, a major 'reward' was issued, such as fleece jackets.

Although the campaign in itself might have been an additional cost on the project, the benefit was immense, because the entire project lost no downtime for accident investigations, stoppages, poor operative performance, etc. The project came in on time and predominantly on its half billion pound budget!

What is the 'Working Well Together' campaign?

The 'Working Well Together' (WWT) campaign is a campaign initiated by the HSE and key construction bodies to improved health and safety throughout the construction industry?

The campaign is underpinned by four key points:

- communication
- commitment
- co-operation
- competence.

The WWT campaign is about recognising and publicising good practice and improvements in health and safety. It can be joined by anyone in the industry from Product Manufacturers to specialist Sub-contractors, Clients and professionals.

Communication is a vital part of the campaign and various methods are used to distribute information across the industry. The HSE and construction advising bodies run seminars, conferences and bus tours on how to improve health and safety in design, construction and maintenance. Leaflets and other newsletters are published.

However, the main information source for the WWT campaign is the website (www.wwt.uk.com) and this is available, free of charge, to anyone who wants to register on the site. Information is provided by the HSE, legislation is explained, and best practice examples are given. Also, every company, from Client, professional to Contractor, that has developed schemes for improving health and safety can present their ideas as Action Plans and these are readily accessible for review or printing. Why reinvent the wheel, when someone else's idea could help with your problem — check out the Action Plans.

Information

Website: www.wwt.uk.com
Helpline: 020 7556 2244

Part 5

Post construction

Chapter summary

Chapter 19 Design Risk Assessments

Liability of the Designer under CDM when a construction phase is finished is the key question dealt with in this chapter.

Chapter 20 The Health and Safety File

What is it, who prepares it, who supplies information, what format should it be in, who keeps it? There are all the common questions raised regarding the Health and Safety File.

19

Design Risk Assessments

Does my liability as a Designer under CDM Regulations finish when the construction project has ended?

No. The CDM Regulations require you as a Designer to consider the future use of the building, including maintenance and cleaning.

You must therefore apply the Hierarchy of Risk Control to future maintenance and cleaning issues, e.g. access to plant and equipment, maintenance activities, cleaning of high-level windows, glass atria, high-level shelving, light fittings, etc.

If an accident were to happen to a maintenance worker, for instance they fell from height, because, as a Designer, you had not provided a safe means of access to their place of work, e.g. no guarded gantry walkway, accessible ladder, etc., then an investigation by either the HSE or the local authority Environmental Health Officer (EHO), depending on the type of premises, could conclude that the accident happened because of poor design principles which did not consider health and safety.

As Designer, you could be interviewed to determine what 'Design Risk Assessments' you carried out on your design and you could be asked to explain how you arrived at the design decision you made.

No legal precedent has yet been set in respect of a Designer prosecution for accidents caused once the building is occupied but as both the HSE Inspector and the EHO become more familiar with applying the CDM Regulations to accident investigations the more likely a test case will be taken.

Designers already have civil liabilities in respect of their designs being 'fit for the purpose' — CDM will impose criminal liabilities.

Legislation

Construction (Design and Management) Regulations 1994

● *Regulation 13*

Code of Practice

Managing Health and Safety in Construction (HSG 224: ISBN 0 7176 2139 1)

Guidance

Designing for Health & Safety in Construction (HSE: ISBN 0 7176 08077)

Who is responsible for ensuring that Design Risk Assessments are provided to the Planning Supervisor?

Designers, Principal Contractors and Contractors all have duties to ensure that the Planning Supervisor is provided with information for the Health and Safety File.

Once the building or structure has been built, the Designer will be responsible for ensuring that the Planning Supervisor is provided with information regarding any residual health and safety risks, in particular, in relation to future maintenance, cleaning and demolition.

Information can be provided in the form of Design Risk Assessments or it can be provided in the form of annotated drawings, detailed specifications, manufacturer's operations and maintenance manuals, and a risk register.

The Principal Contractor must provide design information to the Planning Supervisor in respect of any design detail which either the Principal Contractor or other Contractors have completed on site, i.e. ongoing design details.

If, for example, a specialised Curtain Walling Contractor has installed glazed walls, then there will be design considerations and specifications regarding its stability, erection details, maintenance and cleaning, etc. The specialist Contractor would provide this design information to the Principal Contractor who would pass it on to the Planning Supervisor.

Designers pass information to the Planning Supervisor on design issues, while the Principal Contractor passes information on construction issues.

What information needs to be provided in relation to 'cleaning issues'?

Designers have to consider the health and safety implicates of 'cleaning work' within the structure once it is handed over to the Client as part of their duties under Regulation 13.

'Cleaning work' in respect of design considerations involves the cleaning of any window, translucent or transparent wall, ceiling or roof, in or on a structure where the ceiling involves the risk of a person falling more than two metres.

Information on the design considerations of cleaning parts of the structure involving the risk of falling more than two metres, must form part of the Designer's Risk Assessment and this must be included in the information for the Health and Safety File.

Many accidents occur to employees and maintenance workers once a building is occupied because the Designer 'has forgotten' to design in a safe system of work for reaching surfaces which need to be cleaned.

Designers must give thought to the process and need to design in mechanisms for safe systems of work, e.g.:

- permanent edge protection
- overhead gantries
- vertical cradle systems
- fall arrest systems
- access routes for 'cherry pickers'.

If mechanical systems are unnecessary, then the Designer needs to ensure that they have allowed storage space for stepladders or ladders.

The practical solutions intended to be used by the Designer need to be included in the Health and Safety File. This information should then be accessed by the building occupier's employees or Maintenance Contractors, thereby enabling them to undertake the cleaning work safely.

Legislation

Construction (Design and Management) Regulations 1994

- *Regulation 13*

Code of Practice

Managing Health and Safety in Construction (HSG 224: ISBN 0 7176 2139 1)

20

The Health and Safety File

What is the Health and Safety File as required by the CDM Regulations 1994?

The Health and Safety File provides information that will be needed by anyone who is preparing for construction work or cleaning work on an existing structure, including maintenance, repair, renovation, modification or demolition.

If prepared well, the Health and Safety File should be an invaluable document for all building owners and/or occupiers. It should contain information about the building which is relevant to health and safety.

There is no specific format to the Health and Safety File laid down by the Regulations and it can therefore be in various forms, e.g. paper file, drawings, on computer disk.

The Regulations do not specify the contents of the Health and Safety File except to require that it contains:

- information included with design by virtue of Regulation 13 (2)(b)
- any other information relating to the project which it is reasonably foreseeable will be necessary to ensure the health and safety of any person at work who is carrying out or will carry out construction work or cleaning work in or on the structure or any person who may be affected by the work of such a person at work.

The Approved Code of Practice gives some guidance as to the content of the Health and Safety File as follows:

- record or 'as built' drawings and plans used and produced throughout the construction process along with design criteria

- general details of the construction methods and materials used
- details of the structure's equipment and maintenance facilities
- maintenance procedures and requirements for the structure
- manuals produced by specialist Contractors and suppliers which outline operating and maintenance procedures and schedules for plant and equipment installed as part of the structure
- details and location of utilities and services, including emergency and fire fighting systems
- residual hazards and risks within the structure, e.g. location of hazardous substances and materials, such as asbestos containing materials.

The information to be contained in the Health and Safety File should be agreed between the Client and the Planning Supervisor. After all, the document should provide information for the building owner and they will have a valuable input into describing what information they believe will be relevant. Obviously, not all the Clients will know what to include in the Health and Safety File and in these instances the Planning Supervisor should give advice.

Legislation

Construction (Design and Management) Regulations 1994

- *Regulation 14*

Code of Practice

Managing Health and Safety in Construction (HSG 224: ISBN 0 7176 2139 1)

Guidance

A Guide to Managing Health and Safety in Construction (HSE: ISBN 0 7176 07550)

CDM Regulations — Practical Guidance for Planning Supervisors (CIRIA Report 173)
CDM Regulations — Practical Guidance for Clients and Client's Agents (CIRIA Report 172)

Who prepares the Health and Safety File and where does the information come from?

The Planning Supervisor has to *ensure* that the Health and Safety File is prepared. They do not have to prepare it themselves although it has become a standard part of their responsibilities, expected by most Clients.

Information for the Health and Safety File comes from a variety of sources but key contributors are:

- Designers — the Design Risk Assessments are important particularly where they indicate a 'residual risk' associated with the design
- Planning Supervisor — will have collected important information regarding previous uses of the site, etc., e.g. whether contaminated land is present, environmental hazards, etc.
- Principal Contractor — will have prepared construction sequences for the works, have details of materials and substances used
- Structural Engineers — will have details of load-bearing structures, imposed loadings on floors, guard rails, etc., details and location of foundations
- Building Services Engineers — will have details of plant and equipment, operating and maintenance manuals, location of services, etc.
- Specialist Contractors such as Architectural Glaziers — will have details of types of glazing, fitting details, weight loadings, cleaning methods, etc.

It is the responsibility of the Planning Supervisor to co-ordinate the information to ensure that it is included in the Health and Safety

File. They do not have to write the information, although it would be sensible to compile an introduction and index to the information and detail of where such information is located if not all in one volume.

In many cases it can be extremely practical to have the Principal Contractor compile the Health and Safety File for the project, as they see most of the information at first hand, e.g. the amended drawings which show what was actually constructed and where, Operations and Maintenance Manuals from specialist Contractors, etc.

If the Principal Contractor compiles the Health and Safety File it must be handed over to the Planning Supervisor for checking.

The agreement as to who is responsible for preparing the Health and Safety File must be reached at the beginning of the project. Reference should be made in the Pre-tender Health and Safety Plan as to who is the responsible person, what the Health and Safety File is to contain and how many copies of it there shall be.

Legislation

Construction (Design and Management) Regulations 1994

Regulation 14

Code of Practice

Managing Health and Safety in Construction (HSG 224: ISBN 0 7176 2139 1)

Guidance

A Guide to Managing Health and Safety in Construction (HSE: ISBN 0 7176 07550)
CDM Regulations — Practical Guidance for Planning Supervisors (CIRIA Report 173)

CDM Regulations — Practical Guidance for Clients and Client's Agents (CIRIA Report 172)

What procedures should be followed to put the Health and Safety File together?

If put together properly, the Health and Safety File should be one of the most beneficial requirements of the CDM Regulations.

How often have you taken ownership of a building (even a new house) and not had any idea where the main services are located, whether certain materials have been used or how and when to maintain equipment and service plant? A good, detailed Health and Safety File should include all the information necessary to understand how, what, when, where, and why a building is to be used and maintained safely.

A written procedure and checklist is a good starting point for compiling the Health and Safety File. The following steps could be considered.

- Define who will compile the Health and Safety File.
- Agree with the Client what information they want in the File, how they want it compiled and how many copies are to be produced.
- Discuss with the Designers key information which will need to be included, such as:
  ○ Design Risk Assessments
  ○ details of residual risk
  ○ specific construction methods
  ○ structural details, e.g. floor loadings.
- Agree the procedure for advising the person who is to compile the File, e.g. the Planning Supervisor.
- Discuss with Building Services Consultants/Contractors key information in respect of services which will need to be provided, e.g. Operations and Maintenance Manuals, how many and what format, drawings, etc.

- Advise the Designers and Principal Contractor of additional information which the Client has requested.
- Agree the procedure for site visits to obtain relevant information for the File during the construction phase.
- Obtain a list of all 'Client Direct' appointments and establish what information they may have which will be relevant, e.g. specialist installers.
- Write to all parties outlining the information you require them to provide and the time-scales and deadlines you expect it in.
- Issue reminders through the Principal Contractor and site meeting minutes.
- Discuss with the Client formal procedures for withholding payment of accounts if information is not received.
- Visit the site towards the end of the construction phase and conduct a Hazard and Risk Assessment of the premises to identify information which should be included in the File.
- Agree with the Client a handover procedure for the File, including a time-scale as to when, *realistically*, it will be available after the construction works are completed.

Appendices 19 and 20 outline a written Health and Safety File checklist and on-site Final Inspection checklist for obtaining key health and safety information.

Who keeps the Health and Safety File?

The Client must retain a copy of the Health and Safety File. It must be delivered to him by the Planning Supervisor at the end of the construction works for each structure.

The Client has a duty under Regulation 12 to ensure that any information contained in the Health and Safety File is kept available for inspection by any person who may need information in the Health and Safety File for the purposes of complying with any statutory provisions.

The Client could delegate the responsibility for storing the Health and Safety File to another person, e.g. the Planning

Supervisor or Project Architect, but the statutory duty to ensure that it is available will rest with the Client.

Legislation

Construction (Design and Management) Regulations 1994

- *Regulation 11*
- *Regulation 14*

Code of Practice

Managing Health and Safety in Construction (HSG 224: ISBN 0 7176 2139 1)

Where should the Health and Safety File be kept and how many copies of it should there be?

The Client has to retain a copy of the Health and Safety File in a format that can be used easily by other persons who may need the information.

The information in the Health and Safety File relates to health and safety issues and therefore it is essential that it is readily available, in both location and format, for people using, maintaining or cleaning the building or structure.

A copy of the Health and Safety File should be kept on the premises to which it relates so that it can be easily referenced by staff and maintenance personnel. However, site copies of documents have a tendency to be mislaid and if the Health and Safety File goes missing the Client will not be able to fulfil their duty under Regulation 12.

A practical solution is to prepare two Health and Safety Files — one a detailed Master Copy held at the Client's Head Office, e.g. Property or Legal Department, and a second summary version which contains essential health and safety information for day-to-day use and maintenance of the building within the premises itself.

The information in the Health and Safety File must be accessible to anyone who needs it. This will include Maintenance Contractors. They should be required to consult the Health and Safety File for methods of access to plant and equipment, maintenance procedures, potential hazards, etc. If a copy is not available for them on site and they undertake a task without being made aware of any residual hazards or procedures to be taken and subsequently have an accident, the resulting accident investigation could conclude that had they had access to the information the accident would not have occurred and the Client could be charged with contravening the Regulations. The maintenance company could then sue for negligence in the Civil Courts.

The location, format and numbers of the Health and Safety File should be discussed and agreed between the Planning Supervisor and the Client at the outset of the project. The resulting decisions should be recorded in the Pre-tender Health and Safety Plan.

Legislation

Construction (Design and Management) Regulations 1994

● *Regulation 12*

Code of Practice

Managing Health and Safety in Construction (HSG 224: ISBN 0 7176 2139 1)

Guidance

A Guide to Managing Health and Safety in Construction (HSE: ISBN 0 7176 07550)

Case Study

A major operator and developer of café bars requires the Planning Supervisor to prepare the Health and Safety Files for each and every project, collecting and collating information from all parties as necessary.

The Health and Safety File is prepared in A4 ring binder format so that it is easily accessible and understandable to all persons.

Two copies of the Health and Safety File are produced, one contains all 'as built' drawings and all information, the second contains the same information, excluding detailed as built drawings and as installed drawings.

Mechanical and Electrical Operating and Maintenance Manuals are referenced within the Health and Safety File and a statement in the File requires these manuals to be read in conjunction with the File. However, key health and safety information is copied from the Manuals and included in both Health and Safety Files.

The 'Master' Health and Safety File and full set of Operating Manuals are kept by the Planning Supervisor on behalf of the Client.

The second or 'Site' copy of the Health and Safety File is dispatched to the Unit Manager with covering instructions on how to use it and its importance with regard to health and safety information, safe systems of work, etc.

When the Client disposes of one of the sites, the Client's Solicitors request the onward transmission of the File from the Planning Supervisor to the new owner's Solicitors.

With whom does liability for the Health and Safety File rest?

The Client is legally liable for ensuring that the Health and Safety File is available to any person who may need the information contained within it in order to comply with relevant statutory provisions.

The Client is legally liable for ensuring that the File is transferred to the structure's new owners on disposal of his interests in the 'property of the structure'.

The Client is legally liable for ensuring that leaseholders of any parts of the building have access to the information contained within the Health and Safety File. This may include issuing all leaseholders with a copy but this is not mandatory.

The Planning Supervisor is legally liable for ensuring that the Health and Safety File has been prepared.

The Planning Supervisor is also legally liable for ensuring that the Health and Safety File is 'reviewed, amended or added to' in order to ensure that the information referred to in the Regulations is contained within the File.

The Planning Supervisor is legally liable for ensuring that, on completion of the construction work on each structure included in the project, the Health and Safety File is delivered to the Client.

Liability is straightforward in respect of all responsibilities with perhaps the exception of ensuring that the File is 'amended, reviewed and added to' as placed on the Planning Supervisor.

First reading of the specific requirement placed on the Planning Supervisor under Regulation 14 (e) implies that the Planning Supervisor is responsible for ensuring that the Health and Safety File is accurate and up to date.

At the time of writing, this responsibility has not been tested in the Courts, but it will be if a fatal or major accident occurs which the investigating Inspector determines could have been avoided if the Health and Safety File was up to date.

The duty placed on the Planning Supervisor is 'as far as is reasonably practicable'. It would be unreasonable and impractical to expect a Planning Supervisor to be fully conversant with the detailed knowledge necessary to approve specialist Contractor information. What would be reasonable is to expect the Planning Supervisor to ask the specialist critical questions in respect of health and safety, e.g.:

- has safe access been designed?
- how is access to be gained?
- have any fragile materials been used and, if so, where?
- what hazardous materials/substances have been used, and where?
- what residual risks remain?
- have safety notices been displayed?
- have any hazardous areas been created, e.g. confined spaces?
- what health and safety management systems are recommended to mitigate residual risk?
- what personal protective equipment is expected to be used?
- how and when is maintenance to be carried out?
- how and when is cleaning to be carried out?

The Planning Supervisor should be skilled at picking out unusual and key site-specific health and safety issues and *must* ensure that relevant information is included in the File. A competent health and safety professional does not have to have detailed knowledge of every job task to be able to identify common hazards and risks, and to be able to apply the principles of the Hierarchy of Risk Control to the process.

Legislation

Construction (Design and Management) Regulations 1994

- *Regulation 12*
- *Regulation 14*

Code of Practice

Managing Health and Safety in Construction (HSG 224: ISBN 0 7176 2139 1)

Once the Health and Safety File has been completed and handed over to the Client, who is responsible for keeping it up to date?

The Client retains responsibility for the Health and Safety File once it is handed over to him.

The File will need to be handed over to future Planning Supervisors whenever the Client commissions works which fall within the jurisdiction of the CDM Regulations.

It will be the duty of the Planning Supervisor to keep the File amended, reviewed and added to in respect of all new works. When these works are complete, the File will be handed back to the Client in its amended form.

The Client will need to review carefully whether or not the renovation, repair, redecorating, programmed maintenance, etc., works he commissions fall within the CDM Regulations. Any works involving FIVE or more men on site will fall under the jurisdiction of the Regulations (excluding those works where the Local Authority is responsible). The duty to prepare (or to ensure that it is prepared) the Health and Safety File will fall to the Planning Supervisor. If the Client appoints himself as Planning Supervisor he must update the File himself.

If the works fall outside of CDM, i.e. have less than five workers on site at any one time and are not notifiable, then there is no legal duty on the Client to appoint a Planning Supervisor and therefore no legal duty to prepare, amend, review, or add to, a Health and Safety File.

However, having gone to the not inconsiderable expense of having a Health and Safety File prepared, it seems foolish not to ensure that it is kept up to date as improvement and repair works are undertaken within the building.

There is a growing tendency as buildings change hands for the legal profession to require existing owners to confirm in writing that the Health and Safety File is available and up to date. If a subsequent owner found it to be deficient, they could instigate civil proceedings. Equally, both freeholders and mortgage lenders, e.g. commercial banks, are making the Health and Safety File a legal item in conveyancing and lease drafting work.

Legislation

Construction (Design and Management) Regulations 1994

- *Regulation 12*
- *Regulation 14*

Code of Practice

Managing Health and Safety in Construction (HSG 224: ISBN 0 7176 2139 1)

Guidance

CDM Regulations — Practical Guidance for Planning Supervisors (CIRIA Report 173)

What happens if certain information which should be included in the Health and Safety File is not available?

The information required for the Health and Safety File should be made clear at the beginning of the project, including who is responsible for providing what.

If all the information necessary to complete the File is not available at the end of the construction works, the Planning Supervisor may have to provide an incomplete Health and Safety File to the Client, with details of the outstanding information.

The information which is required for the File is that which is 'reasonably foreseeable will be necessary to ensure the health and safety of any person at work ...'. Certain information may *not* have been reasonably foreseeable during the project and may only be collected retrospectively. This information could reasonably be expected to be excluded from the Health and Safety File when first compiled, but the Planning Supervisor would be expected to 'add to' the File by providing the information as soon as it is available.

Contractors and Client Direct appointments who fail to provide relevant information as requested should be held in breach of contract and financial penalties should be imposed, e.g. retention fees increased to 20% of contract value.

The Planning Supervisor should do all that is reasonably practicable to obtain the information, e.g. contacting Contractors direct, and keep records to that effect.

Those which fail to comply with the requirements to provide information should be judged as lacking either competency or resources to fulfil their obligations under CDM. The Client should be informed of such instances and advice given to 'de-list' the Contractor, etc. The Client could write to the Contractor/company advising them that they will be de-listed.

Contractors will be in breach of Regulation 19 if they fail to provide information promptly to the Principal Contractor. The Principal Contractor will be in breach of Regulation 16 if they fail to provide information promptly to the Planning Supervisor.

Prima fascie evidence of failing to comply knowingly with a legal duty should imply lack of competency and should the Client continue to appoint a Contractor or Designer knowingly, the Client could be held to be in breach of Regulations 8 and 9.

Legislation

Construction (Design and Management) Regulations 1994

- *Regulation 12*
- *Regulation 14*
- *Regulation 16*
- *Regulation 19*

Code of Practice

Managing Health and Safety in Construction (HSG 224: ISBN 0 7176 2139 1)

Case Study

The Electrical Contractor on a project went into liquidation shortly after the completion of the construction works on a new restaurant project, and before the Electrical Operations and Maintenance Manual had been completed and handed over to the Planning Supervisor.

A member of staff was involved in a major, though not fatal, electrical accident and, following the reporting of the accident, the local Environmental Health Officer (EHO) conducted an investigation. He asked for Electrical Test Certificates to verify correct installation of the works under the Electricity at Work Regulations 1989. Those Certificates could not be produced. The EHO shut down the entire kitchen operation until such time as he could be satisfied that the electrics were safe. The Client commissioned another Electrical Contractor to undertake a full test and survey of all of the electrics and to produce the appropriate Test Certificates, together with a suitable Operations and Maintenance Manual. When the subsequent test showed all the electrical wiring installation to be satisfactory, the EHO lifted the Prohibition Notice and the kitchen re-opened. The suspect piece of kitchen equipment was seized for examination.

Had the original Test Certificates been readily available, even not within the premises, the Client would have been able to demonstrate immediately that the electrical installation met all the safety criteria. As the documents were not available, valuable trade was lost for three days — the time taken to organise re-testing and commissioning of all electrical equipment and installations within the premises.

The Client and the Planning Supervisor reviewed procedures for the handing over of key information at the completion of works and agreed that on future projects, unless a copy of the Electrical Installation Test Certificate was provided at the handover meeting or was faxed to the Planning Supervisor prior to the handover meeting, project completion would not be achieved and liquidated damages and other contractual financial penalties would be imposed. The Principal Contractor was held responsible for co-ordinating the information from the Electrical Contractor.

Appendix 1

HSE
Health & Safety
Executive

Notification of project

Note

1. This form can be used to notify any project covered by the Construction (Design and Management) Regulations 1994 which will last longer than 30 days or 500 person days. It can also be used to provide additional details that were not available at the time of initial notification of such projects. (Any day on which construction work is carried out (including holidays and weekends) should be counted, even if the work on that day is of short duration. A person day is one individual, including supervisors and specialists, carrying out construction work for one normal working shift.)

2. The form should be completed and sent to the HSE area office covering the site where construction work is to take place. You should send it as soon as possible after the planning supervisor is appointed to the project.

3. The form can be used by contractors working for domestic clients. In this case only parts 4-8 and 11 need to be filled in.

HSE - For official use only

Client	V	PV	NV	Planning supervisor	V	PV	NV
Focus serial number				Principal contractor	V	PV	NV

---

1 Is this the initial notification of this project or are you providing additional information that was not previously available

Initial notification ☐   Additional notification ☐

---

2 Client: name, full address, postcode and telephone number *(if more than one client, please attach details on separate sheet)*

Name: Telephone number:

Address:

Postcode:

---

3 Planning Supervisor: name, full address, postcode and telephone number

Name: Telephone number:

Address:

Postcode:

---

4 Principal Contractor *(or contractor when project for a domestic client)* name, full address, postcode and telephone number

Name: Telephone number:

Address:

Postcode:

---

5 Address of site: where construction work is to be carried out

Address:

Postcode

Notification of project — continued

6 Local Authority: name of the local government district council or island council within whose district the operations are to be carried out

___

7 Please give your estimates on the following: Please indicate if these estimates are original ☐ revised ☐ *(tick relevant box)*

   a. The planned date for the commencement of the construction work

   b. How long the construction work is expected to take *(in weeks)*

   c. The maximum number of people carrying out construction work on site at any one time

   d. The number of contractors expected to work on site

8 Construction work: give brief details of the type of construction work that will be carried out

___

9 Contractors: name, full address and postcode of those who have been chosen to work on the project *(if required continue on a separate sheet). (Note this information is only required when it is known at the time notification is first made to HSE. An update is not required)*

___

Declaration of planning supervisor

10 I hereby declare that .... *(name of organisation)* has been appointed as planning supervisor for the project

Signed by or on behalf of the organisation .... *(print name)* ....

Date ....

Declaration of principal contractor

11 I hereby declare that .... *(name of principal contractor)* has been appointed as principal contractor for the project. *(or contractor undertaking project for domestic client)*

Signed by or on behalf of the organisation .... *(print name)* ....

Date ....

Appendix 2

How to decide when the exceptions to the CDM Regulations apply

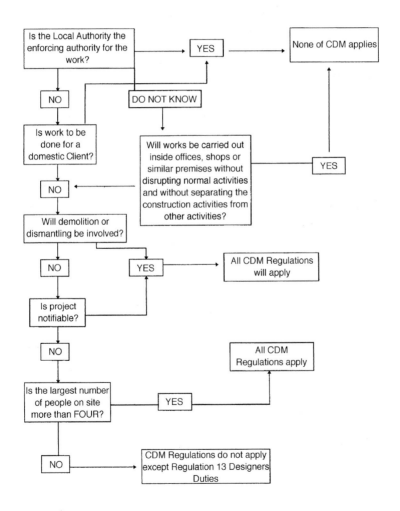

Appendix 3

Client's Agent Questionnaire

Name of company

Name of senior person responsible for overseeing CDM

Nature of organisation

Membership of professional bodies

Individual employee qualifications

Have you performed the role of Client's Agent before?   YES/NO

If yes, please give details

Please give references

Please supply the following:

- Company Health and Safety Policy
- CDM Protocols and Procedures
- Details of how competency and resource issues are dealt with
- Details of Health and Safety Consultants/Adviser Services.

Please supply any further information relevant to your appointment as Client's Agent.

Appendix 4

Formal Appointment of Client's Agent

Formal appointment of Client's Agent — Regulation 4 (4)

*********************** hereby appoint ***********************
****

to act as Client's Agent as itemised in Regulation 4 (4) of the Construction (Design and Management) Regulations 1994 (CDM) in respect of the following projects:

*****
*****
*****
*****
*****

The Client's duties in respect of the CDM Regulations as listed below are specifically transferred.

(*i*)   Appointment of Planning Supervisor to each and every project.
(*ii*) Appointment of Principal Contractor to each and every project.
(*iii*) Assessment of competency and resources of Planning Supervisors and Principal Contractors.
(*iv*) Appointment of competent Designers who are adequately resourced for each and every project.
(*v*)   Provide information to all Planning Supervisors in respect of all projects in relation to health and safety matters, e.g. undertake site surveys to obtain relevant information.
(*vi*) Appointment of contractors, including 'Client Direct' who are competent and adequately resourced in terms of health and safety.

(*vii*) Approval of the Construction Phase Health and Safety Plan *prior* to the commencement of construction works.

(*viii*) Provision and availability of the Health and Safety File to any person who may need to review it. N.B. The Health and Safety File must be handed to ************ at the completion of the project.

************ will be notifying all relevant HSE Offices that their CDM responsibilities have been transferred in accordance with this Agreement.

Signed: ....   Signed: ....

       On behalf of   On behalf of

       Date: ....   Date: ....

Appendix 5

Guidance on what to consider when appointing the Planning Supervisor

The following aspects need to be taken into consideration when the Planning Supervisor is being appointed:

- membership of professional bodies
- construction knowledge, e.g. understanding the process of procurement, specifications, programming, sequence of works, various inter-relationships of trades, etc.
- knowledge of the design process, i.e. understanding design drawings, specifications, design concepts, etc.
- knowledge of health and safety, i.e. the Hierarchy of Risk Control, Risk Assessments, purpose of Method Statements
- knowledge of occupational health and safety issues relative to the future occupation of the building.

Appendix 6

Planning Supervisor Questionnaire

1. Name and address of organisation.
2. Name of head and senior person responsible for overseeing CDM responsibilities.
3. Nature of organisation.
4. Membership of professional bodies:

    (*a*) Corporate membership
    (*b*) Individual(s) membership.

5. Please supply a copy of the organisation's Health and Safety Policy. Ensure specific areas as follows are addressed:

    (*i*)   health and safety arrangements
    (*ii*)   health and safety responsibilities
    (*iii*) health and safety objectives
    (*iv*)   health and safety Risk Assessment procedure
    (*v*)   health and safety training provisions
    (*vi*)   appointment of Competent Person
    (*vii*) safety monitoring and auditing procedures
    (*viii*) health and safety procedures, i.e. guidance on working practices, etc.
    (*ix*)   accident and incident reporting procedures.

6. Please provide examples of accident and incident cases, accident statistics, etc.
7. Please provide specific qualification, training, skills and experience of persons to be engaged as Planning Supervisors on this project.
8. Please provide details of resources available for role as Planning Supervisor. Include estimated number of staff available for professional input, administrative input, etc.

9. Please provide information on resources available in respect of legal and technical information in respect of health and safety, e.g. manuals, codes of practice, books, on-line databases, CD Rom libraries, etc.

10. Please give any details of litigation, arbitration or criminal proceedings in respect of health and safety or environmental protection matters.

11. Please provide evidence of Professional Indemnity.

12. Do you have in-house or external safety expertise available to you?

    If external, please advise name and address and supply details of any contractual arrangements.

    How often do you have access to this external advice?

13. Do you have in-house or external advice on construction methods, project management, construction project costings, resources and time management implications?

14. Have you undertaken any other project work as Planning Supervisor?

    If so, please forward format/protocols, etc. for Pre-tender Health and Safety Plan, Health and Safety File.

Appendix 7

Model Answers to Planning Supervisor Questionnaire

Key points to be included in the answers to questions 1–14 of the Planning Supervisor Questionnaire in Appendix 6.

1. Information as requested.
2. Information as requested.
3. Organisation with experience in design, construction or health and safety essential.
4. Corporation memberships: RIBA
    RICS
    MICEE
    MIOSH
    CITB
    Building Employers' Federation

    Individual memberships: Any of above
    Registered Safety Practitioner

5. Comprehensive Safety Policy required which is specific to the organisation being questioned. Guard against glossy documents that may not be used. Thick lengthy documents do not mean any greater health and safety than thinner documents.

    All points (*i*)–(*ix*) in questionnaire should be included in the Policy.

    Review procedures section to see whether or not good guidance is issued, hazards identified, risks assessed.

6. Accident and incident reports need to demonstrate that accidents and incidents are investigated and preventative measures actioned. What type of injuries are common? Major or minor ones? How many over '3 days' accidents are reported? What is the procedure for reporting notifiable

accidents to the HSE or Local Authority? What about accidents to visitors, public, others. What happens to 'near misses' incidents? Are many treated as important indicators of how to prevent accidents?

7. Qualifications should relate to health and safety, e.g. NEBOSH certificates, diplomas. Membership of Institute of Occupational Safety and Health. Courses on Hazard Identification and Risk Assessment. Training on the 'six pack' of Health and Safety Regulations. Training on confined space entry, breathing apparatus, and other specific areas, e.g. COSHH, electricity, etc.

Skills and experience should be relevant to the project in question, e.g. if the project is the refurbishment of occupied buildings, has the Planning Supervisor experience of such work and the specific hazards and risks.

8. Resources available should be more than one person. Administrative support will be vital for most projects. Access to extra workers. Reliance on self-employed people may not be ideal, etc. Resources necessary will be dependent on the size of the project.

9. Legal and technical information is available from HMSO, HSE books, BSI, etc. Also from trade and industry organisations such as CITB, RIBA, CIRIA, BRE, etc. Information is available in on-line databases, CD Rom, electronically and manually. How is information updated? Do they give any references, e.g. Croner, Sweet & Maxwell, CITB? If information is not kept at source, how easily is it accessible?

10. Details of litigation which should be regarded cautiously would be any that involve health and safety, etc., prosecutions for non-compliance with the law — levels of fines imposed, etc. Information of whether or not Improvement or Prohibition Notices served. Any action under Environmental Protection Act 1990 or Control of Pollution Act 1974 for statutory nuisances. Any undertakings given. Any breaches of Planning and Development Regulations.

11. Professional Indemnity provision needs specifically to cover the responsibilities to be undertaken. The level of cover may be variable depending on project size.

12. If there is an in-house Safety Adviser — who is it, what qualifications, full or part-time, etc.?

If external, is it a recognised Health and Safety Consultancy? What are the contractual arrangements, e.g. one site survey per year may *not* be adequate resources etc.

13. Is there in-house expertise in design and construction or does the Planning Supervisor refer to external advice, e.g to Architects, QS practices, Project Managers? What arrangements do they have? How often can advice be sought? Is it cost specific?

    Is there adequate evidence that the Planning Supervisor will have all-round knowledge of construction phases, cost implications, etc.? Will they be able to understand the project and assess the resources of the Principal Contractor satisfactorily?

14. Evidence of any other commissions as Planning Supervisor should be attached. What type of projects? What value, etc.?

Appendix 8

Questionnaire Appraisal Form (example) — Planning Supervisor

Question	Comment on answer	Potential mark	Actual mark
1		2.5	2.5
2		2.5	2.5
3	Has HSW experience and QS experience	5	5
4	Membership of all relevant professional organisations evident (corporate) Individual memberships high but no RSP nor any membership to IOSH	5	5
5	Safety Policy deficient in six out of nine sections	20	8
6	History of major and minor accidents	20	10
7	No real evidence given of training — references only to 'in-house' training	20	5
8	Established organisations with qualified staff in IT and administration. Available resources	10	10
9	Relies on obtaining information from outside sources. No in-house library in respect of HSW	20	0
10	No litigation history or evidence provided of legal contraventions. However, PI claim progressing in respect of accurate land valuation. However, this is not relevant to HSW etc.	20	15

Question	Comment on answer	Potential mark	Actual mark
11	Full PI cover to £1 000 000 and £5 000 000	10	10
12	External HSW expertise but contract for unlimited access and time. In-house HSW managed by external consultants but relationship in respect of CDM not established	20	10
13	Full in-house advice on construction, costs, etc.	20	20
14	Have yet to undertake major PS role but has supervised minor projects	20	10

ASSESSMENT

Total marks available	200
Actual marks achieved	117
Pass rate	140/200
Questionnaire:	PASS
	(FAIL)

Signed

Client/Client's Agent

Date

ACTION

Further information required on questions: 5, 7, 9, 12, 14

Future re-submission

Acceptable

Not Acceptable

Appendix 9

Project Designer Questionnaire

1. Name and address of organisation.
2. Name of head and senior person responsible for overseeing CDM responsibilities.
3. Nature of organisation.
4. Membership of professional bodies:

   (*a*) corporate membership
   (*b*) individual(s) membership.

5. Please supply a copy of the organisation's Health and Safety Policy. Ensure specific areas as follows are addressed:

   (*i*)   health and safety arrangements
   (*ii*)   health and safety responsibilities
   (*iii*) health and safety objectives
   (*iv*)   health and safety Risk Assessment procedure
   (*v*)   health and safety training provisions
   (*vi*)   appointment of Competent Person
   (*vii*) safety monitoring and auditing procedures
   (*viii*) health and safety procedures, i.e. guidance on working practices, etc.
   (*ix*)   accident and incident reporting procedures.

6. Please provide examples of accident and incident cases, accident statistics, etc.
7. Please provide specific qualification, training, skills and experience of persons to be engaged as Designers on this project.
8. Please provide details of resources available for role as Designers.

Include estimated number of staff available for professional input, administrative input, etc.

9. Please provide information on resources available in respect of legal and technical information in respect of health and safety, e.g. manuals, codes of practice, books, on-line databases, CD Rom libraries, etc.

10. Please give any details of litigation, arbitration or criminal proceedings in respect of health and safety or environmental protection matters.

11. Please provide evidence of Professional Indemnity?

12. Do you have in-house or external safety expertise available to you?

If external, please advise name and address and supply details of any contractual arrangements.

How often do you have access to this external advice?

13. Do you have in-house or external advice on construction methods, project management, construction project costings, resources and time management implications?

14. What record format is in use to detail considerations given to health and safety issues on the project, e.g. written records, CAD information, Risk Assessment forms, computer records, etc.?

15. What procedures do you use of environmental assessment surveys of sites prior to development?

16. Do you have a CDM in-house manual?

17. Has your organisation ever been appointed as Planning Supervisor to any project? Please give examples.

18. Has your organisation developed pro-formas for either Health and Safety Plans or Health and Safety Files?

19. What in-house quality assurance, total quality management or other auditing procedures do you use to demonstrate that formal consideration is given to differing project stages?

20. How have your design techniques and procedures changed so as to accommodate the specific health and safety responsibilities given to Designers under the CDM Regulations 1994?

Appendix 10

Model Answers to Project Designer Questionnaire

Key points to be included in the answers to questions 1–20 of the Project Designer Questionnaire in Appendix 9.

		Potential marks	Actual marks
1.	Information as requested	5	
2.	Information as requested	5	
3.	Organisation with experience in design, construction or health and safety essential	10	
4.	Corporate memberships: RIBA RICS MICEE MIOSH CITB Building Employers' Federation Individual memberships: Any of the above Registered Safety Practitioner	10	
5.	Comprehensive Safety Policy required which is specific to the organisation being questioned. Guard against glossy documents that may not be used. Thick lengthy documents do not mean any greater health and safety commitment than thinner documents. All points (*i*)–(*ix*) in questionnaire should be included in the Policy. Review procedures section to see whether or not good guidance is issued, hazards identified, risks assessed.	10	

	Potential Marks	Actual Marks

6. Accident and incident reports need to demonstrate that accidents and incidents are investigated and preventative measures actioned. What type of injuries are common? Major or minor ones? How many over '3 days' accidents are reported? What is the procedure for reporting notifiable accidents to the HSE or Local Authority? What about accidents to visitors, public, others? What happens to 'near misses' incidents? Are many treated as important indicators of how to prevent accidents? — **10**

7. Qualifications should relate to health and safety, e.g. NEBOSH certificates, diplomas. Membership of Institute of Occupational Safety and Health. Courses on Hazard Identification and Risk Assessment. Training on the 'six pack' of Health and Safety Regulations. Training on confined space entry, breathing apparatus, and other specific areas, e.g. COSHH, electricity, etc. Skills and experience should be relevant to the project in question, e.g. if the project is the refurbishment of occupied buildings, has the designer experience of such work and the specific hazards and risks. — **10**

8. Resources available should be more than one person. Administrative support will be vital for most projects. Access to extra workers. Reliance on self-employed people may not be ideal, etc. Resources necessary will be dependent on the size of the project. — **10**

9. Legal and technical information is available from HMSO, HSE Books, BSI, etc. Also from trade and industry organisations such as CITB, RIBA, CIRIA, BRE, etc. Information is available in on-line databases, CD Rom, — **10**

	Potential Marks	Actual Marks

electronically and manually. How is information updated? Do they give any references, e.g. Croner, Sweet & Maxwell, CITB? If information is not kept at source, how easily is it accessible?

10. Details of litigation which should be regarded cautiously would be any that involve health and safety, etc., prosecutions for non-compliance with the law — levels of fines imposed, etc. Information of whether Improvement or Prohibition Notices served. Any action under Environmental Protection Act 1990 or Control of Pollution Act 1974 for statutory nuisances. Any undertakings given. Any breaches of Planning and Development Regulations.   10

11. Professional indemnity provision needs specifically to cover the responsibilities to be undertaken. The level of cover may be variable depending on project size.   10

12. If there is an in-house Safety Adviser — who is it, what qualifications, full or part-time, etc.? If external, is it a recognised Health and Safety Consultancy? What are the contractual arrangements, e.g. one site survey per year may *not* be adequate resources, etc.   10

13. Is there in-house expertise in design and construction or do they refer to external advice, e.g. to Architects, Quantity Surveyors' Practices, Project Managers? How often can advice be sought? Is it cost specific?
Is there adequate evidence that the Designer will have all round knowledge of construction phases, cost implications, etc.? Will they be able to understand the project and assess the resources of the Principal Contractor satisfactorily?   10

	Potential Marks	Actual Marks
14. Evidence of CAD, Design Risk Assessment Pro-formas, computer records, master manual of risks.	10	
15. Evidence of use of contaminated land surveys, environmental impact assessments, knowledge of EN 1400.	10	
16. Evidence of practical manual with protocols, audit trail, etc.	10	
17. If previously appointed as Planning Supervisor, this should indicate good knowledge of CDM principles and health and safety.	15	
18. Evidence of pro-formas included could be answered in association with 16 above.	10	
19. Evidence of BS 5750/ISO 9000, TQM Systems, Investors in People, etc.	10	
20. Evidence of changing attitude to design issues so that health and safety is adopted within care principles of design.	15	
TOTAL	200	

PASS = 150   ACTUAL SCORE =

PASS/FAIL

Signed: Date:

Planning Supervisor

Appendix 11

Design Risk Assessment

Project address:

Designer:

Design company:

Description of project:

Design activity under assessment:

Hazards identified	Construction	Maintenance/cleaning

Design consideration to eliminate or reduce hazard:

Residual risk:

Control measures necessary:

Information to be relayed to Planning Supervisor for inclusion in:

(*i*) Pre-tender Health and Safety Plan
(*ii*) Health and Safety File

Other relevant health and safety information:

Signed: ....

      (Designer)

Date: ....

Appendix 12

Letter of appointment for Principal Contractor

The Managing Director
Anywhere Builders Ltd
1 The Street
Anytown

Dear Sir

Re: Construction Project: Super Retail Park
   Construction (Design and Management) Regulations 1994

We are pleased to be in negotiation with your Company for the contract to build a new development shell building at the above retail park on behalf of the freeholders, ANC Leisure Plc.

In accordance with the duties imposed on us as Clients under the Regulations, we do hereby formally appoint you and your Company as PRINCIPAL CONTRACTOR for the entire duration of the project. You are therefore required to fulfil all statutory duties pertaining to the appointment.

The Planning Supervisor will be in contact with you regarding completion of the formal notification, F10, which is to be sent to the area HSE office.

Yours faithfully

Appendix 13

Construction Phase Health and Safety Plan Pro-forma

Project details

Address of premises:
Client:
Architect:
Quantity Surveyor:
Structural Engineer:
Building Services Consultant:
Project Manager:

Planning Supervisor:

Principal Contractor:

Project time-scales: State date:
                            Completion:
                            Partial handover dates:

Health and safety objects for the Project

Organisation and management for health and safety on site

Site Agent
Contracts Manager
Health and Safety Manager
Safety Director
Health and Safety Consultants

Emergency procedures

Fire

Explosion, gas release

Building/structure collapse

Major chemical release

Discovery of asbestos or other prohibited substance

Procedures for selecting Contractors and Sub-contractors

Procedures for undertaking Risk Assessments

Procedures for verifying Contractor's Risk Assessments and Method Statements

Procedures for checking Contractor's competency and resources

Site-specific hazards and risks

Who will conduct generic site Risk Assessments?

Site-specific control measures for hazards and risks

Permit to Work system:

Confined space working
Hot Works
Excavations, cofferdams, etc.
Earth moving
Working at height
Work in risers, lift shafts
Working over water
Working with electricity, gas services
Using mobile elevating platforms
Scaffolding
Working with hazardous substances
Vehicle movements

Site set-up

Welfare facilities

Number of toilets
Number of urinals
Number of wash hand basins

Location:

Drying room facilities:

Mess room facilities:

Canteen facilities:

First aid

Location of first aid room

Location of first aid kits

Names of trained first aiders

Welfare facilities for clients and site visitors

Accident/Incident reporting

Who will notify accidents?

What records/systems will be kept on site?

Who will investigate site accidents/incidents?

How will Sub-contractor accidents be dealt with?

How will site personnel be made aware of site safety issues raised by accident reporting?

Site safety management and co-ordination

Daily safety meetings

Weekly safety meetings

Site access arrangements

For operations

For vehicles

For deliveries

Site storage facilities

Site waste disposal facilities

Training

What training will be given?

Who will give it?

Where?

How often?

How will Contractor's and Sub-contractors' safety training be checked?

Who will keep records?

Statutory inspections of equipment

What will be checked?

Who will do it?

How often?

COSHH

How will COSHH Assessments be checked?

Who will provide them?

In what format will they be?

How will use of substances, generation of dust, etc., be controlled on site?

Monitoring and auditing site safety

Who will review health and safety?

How often?

What procedures will be adopted?

Who will audit records?

Who will audit training records?

Site Rules

What Site Rules are envisaged to deal with the following?

1. Working at heights.

2. Excavations.

3. Demolitions.

4. Erecting scaffolding, etc.

5. Using hoists, lifts, cranes.

6. Maintaining 110 v supply.

7. Using portable electrical equipment.

8. Manual handling.

9. Using welding equipment.

10. Hot Works permits.

11. Permit to Work systems.

12. Working with polluted water.

13. Rodent/insect infestations.

14. Temporary support works formwork.

15. Roof works.

16. Removal/installation of glazing.

17. Provision and use of work equipment.

18. Removal of waste

19. Use of hazardous substance.

20. Controlling dust emissions.

21. Controlling noise emissions.

22. Testing and commissioning equipment.

Appendix 14

Checklist for approving a Construction Phase Health and Safety Plan

Does the Plan contain the following?

Yes No Comment

1. General description of project and address.
2. Details of Project Team, Client and Planning Supervisor.
3. Construction time-scales.
4. Statement of health and safety principles and objectives for the project.
5. Site-specific information about working restrictions, environmental matters, e.g. roads, schools, residential area.
6. Management of health and safety on the project, e.g. name of Site Agent, Safety Officer, Director responsible for safety.
7. Details as to how the Principal Contractor will liaise in respect of all matters, but particularly health and safety, with all other Contractors, Sub-contractors and Client Direct appointments.
8. What health and safety standards are to be adopted, e.g. compliance with Regulations, Codes of Practice, Employers' Requirements, Insurance Company Procedures, etc.
9. Details as to how Contractors will be informed about site health and safety matters, e.g. induction training, toolbox talks.

Yes No Comment

10. Details as to how the Principal Contractor will choose Sub-contractors, i.e. how will they assess competency and resources?

11. How will plant and communal equipment be procured and who will do it, who will check it, who will authorise its removal from site, etc.?

12. What arrangements are planned for health and safety meetings with Client, Designers, Contractors, etc.?

13. Details as to what information will be displayed and where. Where will the F10 be displayed?

14. Who will carry out Risk Assessments of site activity? Who will assess Contractors' Risk Assessments? Who will sign off Method Statements? Who should receive this information — when and how often?

15. Details as to how materials will be delivered and where stored, etc.

16. How will hazardous chemicals be handled and stored? Who will do COSHH assessments?

17. What vehicles are intended on site and how will vehicles and operatives be separated? Who will do the Risk Assessments? Who will plan the traffic routes?

18. How will waste be disposed of — what steps are envisaged, where will they be sited?

19. Is a Fire Safety Plan included?

20. What procedures have been included for fire protection, evacuation, etc.?

21. What other emergencies have been considered?

22. Will LPG or other gases be kept on site — if so, where?

23. Will Hot Works be anticipated? Is a test works permit to be used?

24. How will temporary services be provided?

25. Who will ensure existing services are dead, disconnected? What Permit to Work system will operate?

26. How will commissioning and testing be undertaken?

27. What plant and equipment will be provided for communal use? Who will be responsible for checking it?

28. How will accidents and incidents be reported? Who will keep the accident book, first aid kit, etc.? Will there be a trained first aider on site — who will it be? How will they be recognised?

29. What welfare facilities are to be provided and where, e.g. number of toilets and wash hand basins? Where will 'potable' water be available? What messing facilities are to be provided — where will they be?

30. What information and training will be available for people on site — who will provide it, how often, etc?

31. What Site Rules are envisaged?

32. How will health and safety be monitored on site — who will do it, how often? Who will rectify site defects?

33. How will information be collated for the Health and Safety File?

34. Who will conduct the project review?

Appendix 15

Construction Phase Health and Safety Plan Assessment Form

CONSTRUCTION PHASE HEALTH & SAFETY PLAN ASSESSMENT FORM

PROJECT:

PRINCIPAL CONTRACTOR:

CONSTRUCTION SAFETY PLAN:　　　　　　Date received:

Comments:

Compliance with Regulation 15?　　　☐ Yes　☐ No
Can works commence on site?　　　　☐ Yes　☐ No

Approved by: ....　　　.................　　　.............
　　　　　　　Signature　　　　Print name　　　　Date

Notifications (by fax): ☐ Client　☐ Principal Contractor　☐ Architect

Appendix 16

Principal Contractor's Risk Assessment (example)

Project details:	New retail store Any Town Any County
Principal Contractor:	ABC Contractors Ltd
Job activity:	Delivery of materials, plant, equipment to site
Job location:	Rear of premises, adjacent to rear yard and access roadway
Hazards:	Vehicle movement/reversing vehicles Noise Dust Falling objects Restricted access for emergency services Moving/off loading materials, equipment, etc.
Risks:	Being knocked over by vehicle Being crushed by vehicle Being injured by materials as they are off loading, falling objects
Who is at risk:	All operatives, public, other tenants
Likelihood of and severity of risks:	Medium – High
Control measures:	Restrict delivery times to when adjoining shop not occupied Provide Banksman for all deliveries when vehicles need to reverse

Ensure all vehicles have available alarms when
reversing
Provide lifting equipment
Ensure engines turned off during unloading
Provide training to operatives in the area
Introduce a site rule that all Sub-contractors must
notify Principal Contractor's Site Agent of when
and what deliveries are expected
Only one delivery allowed at a time

*Person responsible for
ensuring control
measures completed:*   Site Agent

*Risk Assessment
completed by:*

Date:

Appendix 17

Principal Contractor's Method Statement (example)

Job Activity: Delivery of plant equipment and materials

All Contractors/Sub-contractors will advise the Principal Contractor's Site Agent of the anticipated delivery times and types of delivery expected on to the site.

At least 24 hours' notice is required and Contractors/Sub-contractors are to complete the attached Intended Delivery Note.

All deliveries will be co-ordinated by the Principal Contractor and, where more than one delivery is scheduled at the same time, the Principal Contractor shall decide precedence of deliveries, consulting with each Contractor as necessary. A delivery schedule will be issued at the beginning of each shift.

All delivery drivers are to report to the Site Office. A Banksman will attend on all deliveries and will direct the reversing of all vehicles into the yard. The Banksman will be responsible for ensuring that all operatives, members of the public, adjoining tenants, etc., are kept away from the delivery vehicles. Hazard warning signs may be displayed.

Portable lifting devices will be made available by the Principal Contractor for the removal of materials, etc., All lifting devices are to be checked and maintained by the Principal Contractor.

All engines will be switched off during the delivery process.

Operatives will not be allowed to cross the rear yard during deliveries. Long materials, e.g. joists, steel girders, etc., will be removed by a minimum of two operatives and the access route to the storage area will be kept free of operatives.

Materials, etc., will be stored in designated areas as decided by the Principal Contractor.

The Banksman will ensure clear passage of the departing delivery vehicle.

Appendix 18

Welfare facilities guide – toilets

Sanitary accomodation should be provided as follows.

The Principal Contractor should ensure that sanitary accommodation is available at all times, is accessible to all persons and not obstructed by plant, equipment or other builders debris, etc. It *must* be kept clean, well lit and in working condition. The number of facilities and wash stations to be provided should comply with the table below.

No. of men at work	No. of toilets	No. of urinals	No. of wash stations
1–15	1	1	2
16–30	2	1	3
31–45	2	2	4
46–60	3	2	5
61–75	3	3	6
76–90	4	3	7
91–100	4	4	8
Above 100	An additonal toilet for every 50 (or part) men plus an equal number of additional urinals, plus an additional wash hand station for every 20 operatives		
	Wash hand stations should be provided with adequate supplies of hot and cold running water. Toilets should preferably be wash down water types		

Reference: British Standard 6465: Part 1: 1994, Section 7.6 Table 4

Appendix 19

Health and Safety File checklist

PART 1

Who is to compile the File?
What information is to be included?   Annotate attached list?
How many copies are provided?
In what format?
Where are copies to be sent/held?
Have Designer's Risk Assessments been received?   YES/NO
If no, what is outstanding?
When will such information be available?
Have specialist contractors been contacted with details of information required?   YES/NO
If no, who is outstanding?
Who will be providing Operations and Maintenance Manuals and how many copies?
What information is required from the Principal Contractor?   Annotate attached list

Has information regarding 'Client Directs' been obtained: YES/NO

Attach list of companies contacted.

Have all Contractors and companies been advised in writing
about their responsibilities for providing information in
respect of health and safety matters for the building?   YES/NO

Is the matter of the Health and Safety File and its
contents raised at Site Meetings?   YES/NO

Have procedures for site visits, including 'final inspection'
been agreed with all parties so that information can be
collected?   YES/NO

Has a procedure for communicating on-site design
changes been agreed?   YES/NO

Signed: ....   Date: ....

PART 2

Has all information been received?	YES/NO
If no, what is outstanding?	
Have reminders been sent out?	YES/NO
Have contractual monies been withheld?	YES/NO
Has handover with Client been agreed?	YES/NO
Has File been completed?	YES/NO
Has File been checked, reviewed and updated as necessary?	YES/NO
By whom?	
File handed over to Client on:	
In what format?	
How many copies?	
Have all legal responsibilities been discharged?	YES/NO

Signed: .... Date: ....

Planning Supervisor:

Client acceptance of Health and Safety File

Signed: .... Date: ....
Client:
Position:

Health and Safety File

Contents list
(documents required depending on site)

1. Contaminated land search
2. Asbestos survey
3. Damp proofing certificate/details?
4. Schedule of mechanical services carried out

   Report on what exactly what was installed and location
   Model number and manufacturer of equipment

5. Schedule of mechanical services carried

   Report on what exactly was installed and location
   Model number and manufacturer of equipment

6. Maintenance requirements of new equipment
   (electrical and mechanical)
7. As-built drawings
8. Finished schedule
9. As-fitted drawings
   (electrical and mechanical equipment)
10. Structural specification
11. Building control completion certificate
12. Electrical installation completion certificate
13. Mechanical equipment commissioning details
14. Hazardous areas of the building
15. Cleaning procedures for all areas above two metres
16. Access routes for maintenance purposes
17. Use of fragile materials and location
18. Schedule of substances used
19. Design Risk Assessments for Residual Health and Safety Risks

Checklist of information required for Health and Safety File

Project: .... Builder's completion date: ....
Architect: ....
Principal Contractor: .... Structural Engineer: ....
Electrical Contractor: .... Mechanical Contractor: ....

Date
received

1. Planning permission/consents (*Architect*)
2. Clean Air Certificates following asbestos removal
   (*Architect*)
3. Lift Test Commissioning Certificates (*Architect*)
4. Timber and damp survey and certificate/guarantee
   — to include schedule of materials used (*Architect*)
5. As-built drawings (*Architect*)
6. Building Control Completion Certificate (*Architect*)
7. Drainage test report (*Architect*)
8. Kitchen Commissioning Certificate (*Architect*)
9. Schedule of finishes and materials used (*Principal
   Contractor*)
10. Mechanical commissioning certificates (*Mechanical
    Contractor*)
11. Mechanical Operating and Maintenance Manual
    (*Mechanical Contractor*)
12. Electrical Test Certificates (*Electrical Contractor*)
13. Electrical Operating and Maintenance Manual
    (*Electrical Contractor*)
14. Structural survey (*Structural Engineer*)
15. Structural specification (*Structural Engineer*)
16. Structural hazard assessment (*Structural Engineer*)
17. Structural drawings — as built (*Structural Engineer*)
18. Confirmation that Managers have received on-site
    training (*Principal Contractor, Mechanical Contractor*
    and *Electrical Contractor*)

Appendix 20

On-site final inspection checklist

Information for Health and Safety File

A CONSTRUCTION PROCESS

1. Have any unusual structural works been undertaken?   YES/NO

   ```
   Give details
   ```

2. Has the building been constructed using traditional methods? YES/NO

   ```
   Give details
   ```

3. Have any hazardous construction materials been used, e.g.:

   MDF board?   YES/NO
   formaldehyde insulation?   YES/NO
   carcinogenic substances?   YES/NO

4. Has any asbestos been left on the site in an encapsulated
   condition?   YES/NO

   ```
   Give details
   ```

5. Are hazard warning signs displayed?   YES/NO

B PLANT AND EQUIPMENT

1. Where is the main plant room located?

> Give details

2. Is plant located on the roof?   YES/NO

3. Is edge protection provided?   YES/NO

> If no, give details of safety protection

4. How is plant accessed on the roof?

> Give details

5. Is any access deemed a safety hazard?   YES/NO

> Give details

6. Is any further PPE or safety harnesses required?   YES/NO

> Give details

7. Is access safe to other plant areas?   YES/NO

> Give details

8. Are there any hazards associated with the plant
   rooms/locations? YES/NO

Give details

9. Are all warning signs displayed? YES/NO

10. Are access panels clearly defined? YES/NO

11. Are they easily accessible? YES/NO

Give details

12. Is there any inherent safety concern, e.g. access hatches
    located over stairwells? YES/NO

Give details

13. Are vertical cat ladders, pull-down ladders provided? YES/NO

Give details

14. Is there safe means of access/egress? YES/NO

Give details

C GLAZING

1. What provision has been made during the design process for window cleaning?

Give details

2. How will glazed areas, e.g. domed atriums, be accessed?

Give details

3. Does the building have glazed areas which could be safety hazards, e.g. low level panels in doors, walls, partitions?   YES/NO

Give details

D LIGHT FITTINGS

1. Are light fittings accessible?   YES/NO

Give details

2. What light fittings are inaccessible from a health and safety point of view?

Give details

3. What light fittings, if any, have mechanical/electrical winching devices to allow safe access for cleaning/maintenance?

How/where are the controls accessed?

> Give details

4. Have long-life bulbs been specified?   YES/NO

5. Are there any areas where an unsafe system of work will
   be created by accessing light fittings?   YES/NO

> Give details

6. What about external light fittings?

> Give details

7. If walkways and gantries are provided, do these give safe
   means of access?   YES/NO

> Give details

8. Are all intermediate guard rails and toe boards in place? YES/NO

> Give details

9. Can light fittings be reached safely?   YES/NO

> Give details

E CLEANING

1. What provision has been made for high level cleaning access?

    > Give details

2. What needs to be cleaned above 2·0 m?

    > Give details (including 'bric a brac')

F MAINTENANCE

1. Is all plant and equipment accessible for maintenance
    purposes?   YES/NO

    > Give details

2. Can ductwork be accessed for cleaning and maintenance? YES/NO

    > Give details

3. Can water tanks, etc., be accessed for cleaning and
    maintenance?   YES/NO

    > Give details

4. Can fire alarms, security cameras, etc., be accessed for
    maintenance purposes?   YES/NO

    > Give details

G HAZARDOUS AREAS

1. Do the premises have any areas which could be defined as hazardous?
    Such as:

    confined spaces   ☐
    low headroom areas   ☐
    restricted access areas   ☐
    poor ventilation areas   ☐
    areas with fume build-up   ☐
    high voltage areas   ☐
    pressure systems   ☐
    boiler rooms   ☐
                                   (please tick)

    Give details

2. What health and safety provisions have been made/should be made to
    control exposure to risk?

    Give details

3. Are there any areas external to the building which could
    be hazardous?   YES/NO

    Give details

H ANY OTHER MATTERS WHICH RELATE TO HEALTH AND SAFETY?

    Give details

Alphabetical list of questions